READING JOHN

CASCADE COMPANIONS

The Christian theological tradition provides an embarrassment of riches: from scripture to modern scholarship, we are blessed with a vast and complex theological inheritance. And yet this feast of traditional riches is too frequently inaccessible to the general reader.

The Cascade Companions series addresses the challenge by publishing books that combine academic rigor with broad appeal and readability. They aim to introduce nonspecialist readers to that vital storehouse of authors, documents, themes, histories, arguments, and movements that comprise this heritage with brief yet compelling volumes.

RECENT TITLES IN THIS SERIES:

Reading Augustine by Jason Byassee
Conflict, Community, and Honor by John H. Elliott
An Introduction to the Desert Fathers by Jason Byassee
Reading Paul by Michael J. Gorman
Theology and Culture by D. Stephen Long
Creation and Evolution by Tatha Wiley
Theological Interpretation of Scripture by Stephen Fowl
Reading Bonhoeffer by Geffrey B. Kelly
Justpeace Ethics by Jarem Sawatsky
Feminism and Christianity by Caryn D. Griswold
Angels, Worms, and Bogeys by Michelle A. Clifton-Soderstrom
Christianity and Politics by C. C. Pecknold
A Way to Scholasticism by Peter S. Dillard
Theological Theodicy by Daniel Castelo
The Letter to the Hebrews in Social-Scientific Perspective by David A. deSilva
Basil of Caesarea by Andrew Radde-Galwitz
A Guide to St. Symeon the New Theologian by Hannah Hunt

READING JOHN

CHRISTOPHER W. SKINNER

CASCADE *Books* • Eugene, Oregon

READING JOHN

Cascade Books
An Imprint of Wipf and Stock Publishers
199 W. 8th Ave., Suite 3
Eugene, OR 97401
www.wipfandstock.com

ISBN 13: 978-1-61097-803-3

Cataloging-in-Publication data:

Skinner, Christopher W.

Reading John / Christopher W. Skinner.

xii + 152 p.; 20 cm. —Includes bibliographical references.

Cascade Companions

ISBN 13: 978-1-61097-803-3

1. Bible. John—Criticism, interpretation, etc. I. Title. II. Series.

BS2615.52 S45 2015

Manufactured in the U.S.A.

For Kelly Iverson

CONTENTS

PREFACE

I ALMOST ALWAYS FEEL the same way at the end of a book project. There's an initial sense of satisfaction, accompanied by a wave of exhaustion, all of which is tempered by slight apprehension about putting my ideas out there for public consumption. This is now the seventh book that I have been able to nurture from a vague idea into a fully gestated creation and the combination of excitement and hesitation persists. In my profession one can easily expend a great deal of energy writing for other scholars where lapsing into technical jargon can become almost as effortless as breathing. Throughout this project I have labored to maintain a balance between the substance of biblical scholarship and the task of effective communication. My overarching concern has been to connect with readers who are not experts on the Bible and thereby create a resource that will prove genuinely useful for readers of the New Testament. Most of the illustrations and anecdotes that are included here come directly out of my teaching and preaching of the Gospel of John over the past fifteen years—two tasks to which I have committed a great deal of emotional energy. In many ways, this is the most intensely personal thing that I have written insofar as it incorporates so much that comes out of my own experience with the Gospel of John.

I am truly fortunate to be surrounded by people who help bring the very best out of me as a teacher, scholar, and writer. My colleagues in the Department of Religion at the University of Mount Olive—Tyanna Yonkers, Carla Williamson, and Neal Cox—are wonderful coworkers and conversation partners. I am especially grateful for the friendship that I have with my colleague Hollis Phelps. For the past five years we have shared adjacent offices, a spatial location that has no doubt benefitted me more than it has him. He has patiently listened to me ramble about topics he really doesn't care that much about and has often responded with helpful insights. My daily conversations with him have kept me honest and helped me to become a better thinker and communicator. I also want to thank Michael Gorman, Anthony Le Donne, Nijay Gupta, and Jaime Clark-Soles, each of whom read and commented on portions of this book before I submitted the final manuscript. Tremendous thanks are due to Francis J. Moloney and Greg Carey, both of whom read the manuscript in its entirety and offered extremely helpful critiques. The insights provided by this stellar group have enriched my understanding of the Fourth Gospel and improved this book. The blame for any remaining deficiencies lies solely with me.

My family remains my greatest source of daily inspiration. My wife, Tara and our three children, Christopher, Abby, and Drew add depth and color to a life that would otherwise be deprived of joy. Teaching and writing are intoxicating ways to spend my days, but going home to them every evening provides a fulfillment that can be found nowhere else.

I have had the opportunity to teach through the Gospel of John numerous times in my career, but one class stands out in my mind both for the quality of students and the overall experience. During my last semester teaching at St. Mary's Seminary and University in Baltimore, Maryland (Spring 2010), I had the joy of teaching an advanced Greek seminar on the Fourth Gospel in the Raymond E. Brown room of the Knott Library. For those who do not know, this carefully guarded, climate-controlled room contains the books, journals, and lectures on the Gospel of John that belonged to the eminent Fr. Brown prior to his untimely death. We all felt privileged to breathe in the air emanating from resources used by Brown during his stellar career. As if that wasn't enough, the class was comprised of a group of superstar students that challenged me to bring my very best each week. I want to thank Dr. Frank Dicken, the Rev. Dr. Jason Poling, Msgr. Richard Bozzelli, and Mr. Kurt Pfund, for a stimulating semester that has continued to shape the way I teach the Gospel of John to this day.

It is not an exaggeration to say that this book would not have been written without the encouragement of my friend Karen Reed. About two years into this project, I was overcommitted (a consistent problem of mine) and I had become discouraged at seeing so little progress. When our family visited her home in the summer of 2013 I had already decided that I was going to give up on the book and move on to something else. Throughout that week, Karen continually prevailed upon me to go back to my writing, insisting, "I need to know what you know." With that encouragement, I started working on the book once again. Each chapter has been written specifically with Karen as the imagined audience. Even if no one else benefits from this book, I pray that she will.

It is a privilege for me to dedicate this book to Dr. Kelly Iverson, my friend of nearly two decades. Kelly and I first met during our seminary orientation back in August of 1997. We became fast friends and found ourselves in many of the same courses over the next four years. Together we would go on to spend hours on end in the Texas heat, parking cars at golf clubs, private parties, and restaurants for extra money to pay the bills. At the end of our time in Texas, we would both go on to enroll in the same doctoral program, another sustained period during which we would engage in many meaningful conversations about so many different topics. I have few friends with whom I can intelligently discuss the merits of a cover-two defense and then immediately shift to a discussion of the inherent weaknesses of redaction criticism. Our conversations about the joys and travails of fatherhood have perhaps been the most meaningful to me over the years. We now live more than twelve hundred miles apart, but I have come to cherish our yearly gatherings at professional meetings along with the occasional calls and emails that allow us to catch up. In his day-to-day life, Kelly embodies the very best of what this book is about: thinking at the highest level and communicating with those who want to learn. Over the past eighteen years, his friendship has been a constant source of encouragement and "fresh air" to me, both personally and professionally. I dedicate this book to him with appreciation for his friendship and the hope for many more years of improving as teachers, scholars, husbands, and fathers.

Christopher W. Skinner
Mount Olive, North Carolina
Fall 2014

Chapter 1

READING JOHN

WHERE TO START?

THERE IS AN APHORISM that I like to quote to my students. I have seen various iterations of the saying, but the version I most often recite goes like this: "We do not see things as they are. We see things as *we are*." Every academic year I encounter a new group of students and find myself faced with the task of introducing them to the study of the Bible. The institution in which I teach is located in a rural center of eastern North Carolina, and many of my students come from backgrounds in which the Bible is read and cherished. These students bring with them an understanding of the Bible that often needs subtle nuance, gentle correction, and occasionally, serious deconstruction. Other students have had little if any exposure to the Bible, which means that I must provide them with a completely different foundation for studying the Bible than the former collection of students. I have found that one of the best ways to initiate such a diverse group to the academic study of the Bible is to begin with this admission:

> I have a set of lenses that you can't see but without which *I* can't see. These are the lenses of my

> background and my experiences, my gender and my upbringing, my ethnicity and my education. These lenses shape, color, inform, and even taint my view of the world and my very best attempts at objectivity. This is also true for each of you.

I begin the semester in this way because I want students to strive for objectivity while also realizing that they will never fully achieve it. I want them to embrace their own experiences, backgrounds, and viewpoints while striving both to question and transcend them.

This book is admittedly a product of my lenses. It is therefore imperfect, and to a certain degree both culturally conditioned and socially located, despite my very best attempts to see beyond my limitations. I confess that I see the Gospel of John not as it is, but as *I am*. Thus, this book is not intended to be a final word on the subject, but rather one professor's take on how to read and understand the gospel. Still, I hope that what I have written here will prove useful to those who are interested in studying the Gospel of John, be it in a classroom, a Bible study group, or even on their own. Above all, I want to help others become better, more perceptive readers of the Gospel of John, with an ability to trace the rhetoric of the narrative from beginning to end. With that goal in mind and with a view to preparing readers for what this book attempts to do, the rest of this chapter will be devoted to outlining the starting points that will guide our reading of the Gospel of John.

STARTING POINTS

(1) The Gospel of John was originally written for **a specific audience at the end of the first century**.

It is common for modern people to approach literature—both ancient and modern—without ever asking, "For whom was this originally written?" It is also quite common for people who identify with the Christian tradition to read the New Testament as if Christian believers of any century were the intended audience. These are oversights that beg for correction. One essential starting point when approaching the Gospel of John is the awareness that modern readers are not the originally intended audience. Rather, the audience for whom the gospel was written was likely a community of Jesus-followers living at the end of the first century with a very different language, worldview, thought world, and geographical location than most modern readers—and certainly most readers of this book. While reflecting on our experience with a text is an essential part of the reading process, it is also important for us to ask questions about those for whom the writing was originally intended; this will allow us to understand the message of the Fourth Gospel in new and potentially enlightening ways.

(2) The Gospel of John was **originally written in Greek**.

The trade language of the Roman world during the first century was Hellenistic Greek (also known as *Koinē*, the Greek word for "common"). This is the language in which the entire New Testament was written. While most of the standard English translations convey the message of John's Gospel adequately, there is little doubt that knowledge of the Greek language can serve to inform and enhance the modern reader's experience with the text. Anyone who has studied another language knows there is no such thing as a one-to-one correspondence between one thought world and another. Sometimes it can be very difficult to take an idea as it is expressed in the idiom of one language and faithfully render that idea into another language. A well-known Italian proverb says, *Traduttore traditore* ("translator traitor"), which is roughly translated, "every translator is a traitor."[1] Translators inevitably make interpretive decisions that influence how a given text is read and understood. Throughout this book I will not only make reference to the Greek text of the New Testament, but also to other ancient documents in their original languages. So as to avoid undermining the reader's confidence in his/her preferred English translation, I reference the Greek only when I think it is absolutely necessary to understand the point under discussion.

(3) The Gospel of John is an **anonymous writing**.

The moniker "*according to John*" was apparently applied to this gospel very early—perhaps as early as the second century—but there is no explicit information about the author within the writing itself. Though all four gospels were originally anonymous, each came to be associated with a specific author over time. The traditional view is that the author was John, the son of Zebedee, one of Jesus' twelve disciples. This view also identifies the anonymous "beloved disciple" (13:23; 19:26; 20:2; 21:7, 20) with the author. Even though it has achieved an almost authoritative status among many modern Christians, this view has been roundly rejected by most contemporary scholars. Not only do we not know who wrote the gospel, but it is also very likely that the gospel was edited multiple times before the final version began to

1. It is interesting to note that even with this proverb we are forced to give a literal translation of the Italian phrase, followed by a translation that serves to explain the meaning more faithfully in idiomatic English.

circulate.[2] Throughout this book I will use the terms John, John's Gospel, and the Gospel of John, all in accord with an established scholarly convention. However, I do not intend these designations to affirm anything about the authorship of the gospel.

(4) The Gospel of John is **an autonomous narrative** that must be read **on its own terms.**

Many different presentations of Jesus exist in contemporary culture and this was also true during the first century; we need only look at the four gospels of the New Testament to confirm this. It is common for many to read the four gospels in light of one another, to read in light of the rest of the NT, or even to read in light of a certain theological system or confession. The Gospel of John is a story of Jesus than can stand on its own without the assistance of other gospels (e.g., Matthew, Mark, Luke, Thomas, etc.) or various interpreters of Jesus' life and vocation (e.g., Paul, James, Augustine, Aquinas, Luther, etc.). Only after we have understood John's unique message about Jesus can we introduce other interpretive voices from the first century or later.[3] This book will look at the unique story of Jesus as it

2. In John 21:24, the Beloved Disciple is identified as the source behind and the author of the gospel. Commentators have not widely disputed the first claim, but, as Michaels affirms, have found the second claim "the more difficult one to accept. . . . That this Gospel in particular, with its presumed late date, its extraordinarily high christology, and its extensive deviation from earlier Gospel traditions, could be the work of an eyewitness, the closest of all the disciples to Jesus, strains credulity in the eyes of some" (Michaels, *Gospel of John*, 1054–55).

3. It goes without saying that my own reading of John has been influenced by "other interpretive voices," so I do not wish to pretend that the reading presented in this book is free from the interpretive

is told in John's Gospel. We cannot fully appreciate how the writings of the New Testament relate to one another until we have understood the distinctive voice of each. Thus, one goal of this book is simply to "let John be John."[4]

(5) There is **no such thing as a "plain reading"** of the Gospel of John.

Though I have already touched on this above, I want to be clear that objectivity is ultimately a myth. When we come to the text we bring ourselves—all of us—to the text. When we study the Bible we pursue an ideal that is practically unachievable: we want to know *what the text is saying, what it means.* If we are going to read the Gospel of John honestly, we must recognize that each of us brings a great deal to the text. What we bring to the text is often as determinative in finding meaning as what we actually find in the text. More often than not, what we bring to the text is the most decisive factor in determining meaning, whether we realize it or not. As I stated above, we must all recognize the influence of our lenses while seeking to transcend them.

Now that we have laid out the assumptions that will guide our approach, we can proceed to an examination of the gospel itself. Since this book is intended to be a critical introduction for students and lay readers, its primary aim is to provide a strategy for interpreting the gospel in an informed way. The next seven chapters move systematically through issues that must be considered when attempting to

choices of others. This book is, as I have already said, a product of my own lenses. However, I am doing my best here to provide a literary-historical reading of the text that respects the gospel's autonomy.

4. See Dunn, "Let John Be John," 309–39.

read the Gospel of John. Chapter 2 sets the stage for everything else that follows. There we discuss the importance of John's Prologue (1:1–18), and how to read the entire gospel in light of its introduction. In chapter 3 we look at the two-level drama that unfolds in the narrative—a conversation that draws upon Starting Point 1 above. Chapter 4 will then consider the interesting and potentially troublesome issue of the gospel's connection to and interaction with first-century Judaism. In chapter 5 we examine the distinctive language used throughout the narrative and what this language communicates about the gospel's Christology. Chapter 6 takes an in-depth look at how John constructs characters and how those figures contribute to the overall rhetoric of the narrative. Since the ultimate goal of this book—as indicated by its title, *Reading John*—is to help others read the gospel effectively, there is a seventh chapter in which we pull together insights from the previous chapters and demonstrate how to read a selected passage from the narrative. The final chapter of this book reflects briefly on contemporary theological concerns raised by an informed reading of this important ancient text.

Chapter 2

JOHN'S PROLOGUE

THE INTERPRETIVE KEY FOR READING THE GOSPEL OF JOHN

When I was in elementary school, my grandparents moved from our hometown in southeastern Virginia to a retirement village in central Florida. For many summers after that, my twin sister and I would visit them and spend a week or two bouncing around Disney World, Epcot Center, Baseball City, and other Orlando-area attractions. Every day had a rhythm of its own, though the schedule remained fairly static. In the mornings we would tackle the theme park circuit and in the afternoons we would return to the air-conditioned house where my grandfather and I would spend several hours watching detective shows until dinner. My grandfather was a big fan of the detective genre and the daytime programming schedule accounted for that perfectly. Our afternoon viewing included such classics as *Baretta*, *Cannon*, *Ironside*, *Barnaby Jones*, *The Rockford Files*, and *Murder She Wrote*. Once a show began, Granddaddy immersed himself in solving the crime and would often interrupt the show to predict the identity of the perpetrator. He was skilled in reading the subtle cues, analyzing the evidence, and tracking down the culprit, and when he called out the bad guy he was nearly always right. Whenever Granddaddy solved the mystery before the show's main character, he would beam with pride at his superior mystery-solving abilities.

Without exception, the most memorable detective program we watched together during those summers was *Columbo*, a show about a homicide detective with the Los Angeles Police Department. What made *Columbo* so memorable for me was how drastically it differed from the format of other detective shows. With most detective shows the viewing audience has a limited amount of information about the crime—generally as much as the characters in a given episode—so that the viewer's challenge is to solve the crime before the detective does. By contrast, the first segment of *Columbo* is always devoted to revealing the crime in detail. The audience witnesses the murder, knows the identity of the perpetrator, and understands the motivation for the crime. This information places the audience in a position of privilege, while Detective Columbo is, by contrast, relatively in the dark. He has not seen the murder take place. He does not know how or why the crime was committed. He arrives on the scene as a blank slate and the audience watches him struggle to discover what has already been revealed. As he stumbles and fumbles his way to solving the crime, we cannot help but be amazed at his sleuthing abilities.

Reading the Gospel of John is an experience not unlike watching *Columbo*. John's story of Jesus begins with a lengthy Prologue (1:1–18), in which the reader is provided with comprehensive inside information about the origins, identity, and mission of "the Word" (1:1, 14), a figure subsequently identified as Jesus Christ (1:17). The Prologue reveals to the reader information that is necessary to evaluate the unfolding events in the story. By contrast, the numerous characters that appear in the story do not have access to the same information that has been revealed in the Prologue. Consequently John's characters often fail to grasp what are, for the reader, basic truths about Jesus' origins, identity, and mission. Much like the first extended scene in every episode of *Columbo*, John's Prologue places the reader in a position of privilege while the characters in the narrative remain in the dark. Throughout the story John's Jesus is faced with a spate of characters that continually struggle to come to terms with information that has already been revealed to the reader in significant detail. The reader is thus fully prepared to watch various characters fail in their understanding of Jesus,[1] undergo progressive epiphanies,[2] and even express the truth about him.[3] Like the moviegoer at a horror film who knows that a crazed madman is on the other side of a door even when the madman's next victim

1. In ch. 3, Nicodemus enters the scene as a seemingly sympathetic character. He is introduced as a prominent figure among the Jews (v. 1) and begins by confessing that Jesus is a teacher who has come from God (v. 2). However, throughout the remainder of his conversation with Jesus he descends into ever-greater levels of incomprehension until his final words in this initial scene are, "How can this be?" (v. 9). Nicodemus appears two more times in the narrative (chs. 7 and 19) and though he appears to progress in his understanding of Jesus, in ch. 3 he is perhaps the paradigm of a misunderstanding character in John's Gospel.

2. In John 4, the Samaritan woman—in contrast to Nicodemus—does not initially appear as a sympathetic character. She is a marginalized, anonymous woman who steadily progresses in her understanding of Jesus. She begins with disdain toward Jesus (vv. 9–12), moves to curiosity about him (vv. 15–19), and ends up wondering aloud if Jesus could be the long-expected messiah (vv. 28–29).

3. Scholars have long recognized that the figure known as the "disciple whom Jesus loved" is the one character who "gets it right" throughout the gospel. This figure, regularly referred to as the "Beloved Disciple," consistently responds to Jesus in ways that are regarded as legitimate from the perspective of the story's narrator. This topic will be discussed in greater detail in chapter 6.

does not, the reader of John's Gospel is able to anticipate movements in the narrative that are altogether unknown to the story's characters. Once we come to terms with this storytelling technique, we are better able to read the Gospel of John on its own terms and are further permitted to enter the world of the text, letting the narrator tell his own story of Jesus apart from the outside interruptions of other first-century interpreters of Jesus.[4]

Numerous terms and concepts are introduced in the Prologue and reappear throughout the

TABLE 2.1

The Septuagint: The Old Testament for a Greek-Speaking World

The Septuagint is a Greek translation of the Hebrew Bible and several other related texts, completed between the 3rd and 2nd centuries BCE. The name is derived from a Latin term, *Septuaginta*, meaning "seventy," based upon a tradition that 70 men were responsible for the translation. For this reason, scholars use LXX—the Roman numeral for 70—as a shorthand when referring to the Septuagint. By the late 4th century BCE, Greek had become the trade language of the civilized world, largely due to Alexander the Great's policy of "forced Hellenization" (i.e., forcing subjugated peoples to adopt all elements of the Greek lifestyle). The Septuagint became the most commonly used form of the Old Testament and served as the authoritative Scriptures for most writers in the New Testament, including the author of John's Gospel.

For more on the significance of the Septuagint, see Timothy Michael Law, *When God Spoke Greek: The Septuagint and the Making of the Christian Bible*.

4. For more on this, see Starting Point 3 in the opening chapter of this book.

story in both character interactions and in Jesus' theological discourses. These concepts provide the necessary foundation for the audience's knowledge of Jesus' origins, identity, and mission. In what follows, I provide a basic sketch of the Prologue with the goal of setting us on the path to reading the Gospel of John as an autonomous narrative with its own unique message about Jesus.

John 1:1–5: The Origins of the Word

> 1 In the beginning was the Word, and the Word
> was with God, and the Word was God. 2 He was
> in the beginning with God. 3 All things came
> into being through him, and without him not
> one thing came into being. What has come into
> being 4 in him was life, and the life was the light
> of all people. 5 The light shines in the darkness,
> and the darkness did not overcome it. (NRSV)[5]

The first words of John's Gospel—"in the beginning" (Greek: *en archē*)—represent a transparent allusion to the creation account in Genesis 1. In the Septuagint (see table 2.1), or Greek translation of the Hebrew Bible, the book of Genesis begins with the identical phrase, and as we move forward in the Prologue it is difficult to escape the conclusion that John's story of Jesus is meant to be situated within the broader story of Israel's God as recounted in Genesis and Exodus.

Throughout the early chapters of Genesis, the God of Israel is shown creating, sustaining, and entering into covenant with humanity. Just as the first creation account[6] takes place

5. Most biblical quotations are from the NRSV. Those not marked as such are my own translation.

6. Genesis contains two distinct creation narratives that are comprised of different sources and provide very different accounts of the origins of the world. When I write of the "first" creation narrative I am distinguishing Gen 1:1—2:3 (the first account) from Gen 2:4–25.

"in the beginning" where God creates by *speaking* light, land, sea, and all living creatures into existence (see Gen 1:3–31), so the Gospel of John pictures *the Word* (Greek: *Logos*)[7] as the one through whom everything was created (1:3). Further, the Word is both the purveyor of life and the light of humanity which shines forth into the darkness (1:4–5). These parallels, which are more clearly seen if one has a working knowledge of the Greek language, are illustrated in table 2.2 below. Given the similar vocabulary as well as the broader concepts at work, it is difficult to ignore the intentional connections drawn between Genesis 1 and John 1.

Table 2.2

Genesis 1: (Septuagint/Greek Old Testament)	**John 1: (Greek New Testament)**
1:1: "In the beginning" (*en archē*)	1:1: "In the beginning" (*en archē*)
1:3: "God said" (*legō*)	1:1, 14: "the Word" (*logos*; the noun form associated with the verb *legō*)
1:3: "Let there be light" (*phōs*)	1:4–5: "that life was the light (*phōs*) of humanity...the light (*phōs*) shines in the darkness"
1:20–24: God creates living creatures: • *psychōn zōsōn* (1:20) • *psychē zōōn* (1:21) • *psychē zōsan* (1:24)	1:4: "in him was life" (*zōē*; the noun form associated with the adjective forms used in Gen 1:20–24)

7. Since the term *Logos* was an important principle in Greek philosophy, many past interpreters assumed the Gospel of John was written for a Greek audience. Today, however, it is more common to assert that John has been written for a more Jewish audience and the *Logos* is somehow connected to the account of God speaking in Genesis 1.

These first few verses detail the origins and creative activity of the Word but also speak to the Word's identity, a much more complex issue for the modern reader in light of the history of Christian interpretation. When faced with the phrase, "the Word was God" (1:1c), many devotional readers of the Bible are quick to equate this statement with a fully orthodox, Christian confession of Jesus' identity, but this would be a mistake. The contemporary Christian understanding of Jesus draws upon what is known as the "Chalcedonian definition" (see table 2.3). The confession established by the Council of Chalcedon (451 CE) details the dual nature of Jesus, also known today as the "hypostatic union." This confession sees Jesus as both fully divine and fully human at the same time. While it is safe to say that the conceptual basis for the Chalcedonian definition was strongly influenced by the Gospel of John, the reverse is not likely. In fact it is quite unlikely that this highly developed theological construct was available within the thought world of the author. Here we are presented with a common challenge and an opportunity to read the Gospel of John with greater clarity and attention to detail. We cannot assume that a widely held, contemporary theological view is found in its fully developed form in the pages of the New Testament. This is an error commonly made by the casual or devotional reader of the Bible, and while it is understandable, it begs for serious correction.

The evolution of Christian devotion led to the development of many theological doctrines, and while the New Testament served as the source material for those developments, the authors of the New Testament worked with the ideas and assumptions of their time. The Gospel of John was likely written by a Jewish follower of Jesus living toward the latter part of the first century CE (ca. 95–100 CE).

Given the particulars of this context, it is difficult to imagine a first-century Jew conceiving of Jesus as both fully divine and fully human at the same time. Rather, this view took several centuries of Christian reflection to crystallize. Thus, the phrase, "the Word was God" should not be regarded as a full statement of Chalcedonian Christology.

Table 2.3

The Chalcedonian Definition

The Chalcedonian Definition was adopted by the ecumenical Council of Chalcedon in 451 CE. The definition reads in part:

"We . . . teach people to confess one and the same Son, our Lord Jesus Christ, *the same perfect in Godhead and also perfect in humanity*; *truly God and truly human*, of a reasonable soul and body; consubstantial with the Father according to the Godhead, and consubstantial with us according to the Personhood; in all things like unto us, without sin . . . *to be acknowledged in two natures* . . . the distinction of natures being by no means taken away by the union, but rather the property of each nature being preserved, and concurring in one Person and one Subsistence, not parted or divided into two persons, but one and the same Son, and only begotten God, the Word, the Lord Jesus Christ."

Nearly all orthodox expressions of "Christology" (i.e., theological formulations about the nature of Jesus) within modern Christianity confess that Jesus was fully divine and fully human at the same time. While there is little dispute that the presentation of Jesus found in the Gospel of John was foundational to the development of this view, it would be a mistake to assume that this complex idea is what the author of John's Gospel had in mind. Such a construct assumes categories of thought that would have been completely foreign to a Jewish follower of Jesus living in the latter part of the 1st century CE.

For our purposes, we understand John 1:1c and similar passages in the gospel as signifying that Jesus is the unique representation of the Father to humanity. In other words, all the realities of Israel's God are fully and mysteriously present in him.[8] To affirm more than this would be

TABLE 2.4
Does John Have an "Anti-Baptist Polemic"?

This question was raised during a period of NT research dominated by a methodology known as "form criticism." The program of the form critics included isolating various orally-transmitted units of gospel tradition and assigning them to different stages of the gospel's development. Against that backdrop, scholars believed they could locate various levels of polemic (a sustained argument against something) and apologetic (a sustained argument in favor of something) in the canonical Gospels. The other NT Gospels present John the Baptist in a substantially positive light. John baptizes Jesus (Mark 1:9–11; Matt 3:13–17; Luke 3:21–22), and Jesus speaks highly of him (Matt 11:11; 17:12–14). Luke goes so far as to insist that John and Jesus are biological cousins (see e.g., Luke 1:39–45), though this is not supported elsewhere in the NT. By comparison, in the Gospel of John Jesus is not baptized by John or anyone else. John also indicates twice that he does not know Jesus (1:31, 33) and later comments, "He must increase and I must decrease" (3:30). Not only does John the Baptist cease to play his seemingly "usual" function—baptizing—he insists over and over that Jesus is greater than he is. When comparing the gospel traditions with one another, some commentators have concluded that the Gospel of John is relentlessly hostile in its presentation of John the Baptist. However, in keeping with our strategy of "letting John be John," I suggest that this conclusion would be difficult to reach if we read John as an autonomous narrative without outside interruptions from the Synoptic Gospels.

8. See the helpful rendering of the NEB: "and what God was the Word was."

unwarranted given the limitations of the author's historical, social, and religious contexts.

In 1:5 we read that "the light shines in the darkness and the darkness has not overcome (Greek: *katelaben*) it." Here the Greek verb *katalambanō* likely has a double meaning, though most English translations are forced to settle for one term over another.[9] When dealing with double entendre, it can be difficult for a modern translator to convey the intended ideas with an economy of words. The verb *katalambanō* is often used of "overcoming through victory" or "making something one's own possession," but it can also be used of processing information as in "to understand" or "to grasp." Throughout the story, the reader encounters instances in which both of these nuances emerge and prove the statement in 1:5 to be true.

For example, characters approach Jesus *by night* and display an inability to *comprehend* elements of Jesus' origins, identity, and mission (see e.g., Nicodemus in ch. 3, the arresting party in ch. 18).[10] The cover of darkness in these

9. The NRSV and ESV read "overcome" with no alternative option. The NIV has "overcome" with an accompanying note that reads, "Or *understood*." Both the NASB and NKJV read "comprehend" with an accompanying note; the note in the NASB reads, "Or *overpower*," and in the NKJV it reads, "Or *overcome*." Perhaps the most interesting modern English rendering is found in the New Living Translation (NLT): "and the darkness can never extinguish it," with a footnote that reads, "Or *and the darkness has not understood it*."

10. Nicodemus comes to Jesus by night (3:1–2), a description which not only represents his darkened understanding but anticipates his complete bewilderment at Jesus' teaching (see 3:9, "how can this be?"). He comes to Jesus, the light of humanity, under the cover of darkness and leaves without comprehending the substance of his words. In a very real sense, the audience's first experience with Nicodemus confirms the truth of the narrator's words: "the darkness has not *understood*" the light (cf. 1:5). In ch. 18, a delegation of temple police and Roman soldiers arrives in the garden at night to arrest Jesus. In 18:3 the delegation is pictured with lamps and torches—two

episodes symbolically represents a darkened understanding. Scenes such as these validate the claim that the darkness has not *understood* the light.

The nuance related to "overcoming through victory" is also evident as the powers of darkness—symbolically represented by opposition to Jesus and by death itself—are not able to *overcome* Jesus, as he both defeats death and emerges bodily from the tomb. In very concrete ways throughout the narrative, human and non-human representatives of darkness are unable either to comprehend or to overcome Jesus, the light of humanity. This type of double meaning is a hallmark of John's writing style, as we will see in subsequent chapters.[11] In these first five verses the reader is exposed to ideas and terminology that will emerge again and again throughout John's story of Jesus.

John 1:6–13: The Word and the World

> 6 There was a man sent from God, whose name was John. 7 He came as a witness to testify to the light, so that all might believe through him. 8 He himself was not the light, but he came to testify to the light. 9 The true light, which enlightens everyone, was coming into the world. 10 He

sources of illumination—in order to take the light of humanity into custody. The group boldly seeks Jesus but when he identifies himself ("I am," v. 5), the delegation falls back into a quasi-worship posture (v. 6)—a response that is ironic and admittedly difficult to understand apart from the reader's knowledge about Jesus' origins and identity. The delegation takes Jesus into custody only because he allows it to happen; he exercises control over the situation from start to finish. Here is a situation in which the darkness does not *overcome* the light. It is up to the reader to make these subtle connections and thereby test the truthfulness of the Prologue's witness to Jesus Christ.

11. Double entendre and other distinctive features of Johannine language will be discussed in detail in chapter 5.

> was in the world, and the world came into being through him; yet the world did not know him. 11 He came to what was his own, and his own people did not accept him. 12 But to all who received him, who believed in his name, he gave power to become children of God, 13 who were born, not of blood or of the will of the flesh or of the will of man, but of God. (NRSV)

The second unit of the Prologue begins with a reference to John the Baptist, though the title "the Baptist" never appears at any point in the Gospel of John.[12] For many readers of the New Testament, John's appearance here will come as little surprise, since he is one of the first characters introduced in all three Synoptic Gospels. In both Mark and Matthew, John is among the first characters to speak. In the Gospel of Luke, the narrative begins with an introduction to John's parents and the miraculous circumstances surrounding his birth. He is a key figure in all four NT Gospels. However, the picture of John the Baptist in the Gospel of John differs significantly from his presentation elsewhere. This recognition provides yet another reminder that we must read each gospel on its own terms before introducing other first-century interpretations of Jesus' life and ministry.

In 1:6 we learn that John has been *sent from God* (Greek: *apestalmenos para theou*), a description that is important for the unfolding story since Jesus is the only other character in John's story described as "sent from God."[13]

12. In Mark 1:4, John appears with the descriptor *ho baptizōn* ("the one who baptizes"). In Matthew 3:1, John is called "the Baptist" (*ho baptistēs*)—a title which also appears in Luke 7:20, 33; 9:19. The Fourth Gospel simply refers to him as John, though the narrator does include information about him performing baptisms (see 1:24, 26, 28, 33).

13. "Sending" is an important theme in the narrative and great attention is given to Jesus' role of a representative "sent by God" (see 4:34; 5:23–38; 6:29–57; 7:16–33; 8:16–42; 9:4; 10:36; 11:42; 12:44–49;

This revelation about John's origins creates a subtle link that will serve to connect the public careers of the two teachers. The next few verses clarify John's status vis-à-vis Jesus. John is not the light but rather a witness to the light (vv. 7–8). He testifies to the true light in order to engender belief in the one who enlightens all humanity. We see that John has no messianic status—something John will later admit when he is questioned publicly (1:19–21)—though he has been authorized by God to bear witness to Jesus.

In the view of some scholars, John's testimony about himself and the narrator's description of him are two pieces of a wider "anti-Baptist polemic" found in multiple places in the Gospel of John. This view is rooted in a much different approach to interpreting the NT Gospels than what we have been advocating here (see table 2.4). Our reading of the gospel sees the presentation of John the Baptist as substantially positive. It is true that John consistently points away from himself and toward Jesus, but this should not be regarded as problematic in light of the gospel's primary interest. Jesus is the central figure of the Fourth Gospel and all activities and character interactions necessarily revolve around him. John's appearance in the all-important Prologue, along with the affirmation that he has been "sent by God" is an indication to the reader that he has been commissioned as a reliable representative of the same God who has also sent Jesus. As such, John's subsequent testimony about Jesus as the "Lamb of God" (1:29, 36) and "Son of God" (1:34)[14] will prove to be reliable and will provide the

13:20; 14:24; 15:21; 16:5; 17:3–25; 20:21).

14. Most English translations read "Son of God" in John 1:34, but there is a variant reading, "God's chosen one" (*ho eklektos tou theou*), which I am personally persuaded is the better reading. I have chosen to retain "Son of God" here since it is more familiar to most non-specialist readers of John's Gospel. For more on my departure from the reading "Son of God," see my article "'Son of God' or 'God's Chosen One' (John 1:34)?"

Table 2.5

Jesus and Jewish Feasts in the Gospel of John

The important religious festivals of the Jewish calendar year make numerous appearances in the Gospel of John. Often, the holidays serve as the occasion for one of Jesus' miraculous deeds.

1. Passover (2:13; 6:4; 11:55—19:42)
- Commemorates YHWH's protection of Israel's firstborn just prior to the Exodus from Egypt.
- Background reading: Exodus 11–13.

2. Tabernacles (7:2)
- Commemorates YHWH's protection of and provision for Israel during their wilderness wanderings. Specifically looks back to the temporary tents the children of Israel lived in during that period.
- Background reading: Exodus 23:16; Leviticus 23:34–36, 39–43; Numbers 29:12–38; 31:10–13.

3. Dedication (or Hanukkah) (10:22)
- Commemorates the rededication of the Jewish temple in 164 BCE
- Background reading: 1 Maccabees 4:56–59; 2 Maccabees 10:6–7.

4. "A Feast of the Jews" (5:1)

reader with further necessary information about the identity and mission of Jesus.

In 1:10 we read of the relationship between the Word and "the world" (Greek: *kosmos*). In Hellenistic Greek, *kosmos* is a complex and multilayered term that carries a range of meanings, several of which are used in the Gospel of John. The narrator uses *kosmos* to refer to the material reality of the created order (e.g., 1:10b), the physical realm into which Jesus has entered (e.g., 1:9, 10a; 3:17, 19; 6:14),[15] and the object of God's affection and salvific intentions (e.g., 1:29; 3:16, 17c; 4:42; 6:51).[16]

Also significant for John's theological presentation is the use of "the world" as a symbol for wayward humanity.[17] These various nuances help to create a sharp dichotomy between the ethos of the realm above—the place from which Jesus has come—and the ethos of the realm below. In short, in the Gospel of John the term *kosmos* is used of a place, a people, and a general attitude of opposition to God. The reader must pay close attention to the ways in which the term "world" is used so as to distinguish between the nuances operative in a given context.

As a means of laying the groundwork for one of the Gospel's major themes—the rejection of Jesus—the narrator continues by commenting that the Word came to his own place (i.e., the world as physical realm) and his own people (i.e., humanity) did not receive him (v. 11). Against the backdrop of the previous verse which details the Word's rejection by the world, this verse provides further confirmation that the world is hostile toward the Word. As the agent of God's creation (see 1:3), the Word is the generative force behind everything that exists. Thus, it is appropriate to refer to the world as "his own place" and all of humanity as "his own people." The Word has come into the world he created and that world presently suffers from a darkened perspective. Such darkness renders humans unable to understand

15. The Fourth Gospel presents Jesus as the one who has come "from above." Thus, his departure from the Father represents his entrance into "the world," the realm of "below."

16. See, among others, 1:29; 3:16, 17c; 4:42; 6:51.

17. The assumption of a "fallen" humanity would continue to fit within the wider story of Israel's God as told in Genesis 3.

the Word and openly hostile toward his mission (see 1:5). Despite this existential reality, there are some who will recognize the Word for who he truly is, call upon his name,[18] and become a part of God's newly constituted family—a family built solely by God's initiative (see vv. 12–13). The authority to confer the status, "child of God," has also been granted to the Word. These children are new creatures born not as a result of human sexual relations. They are (re)born by God's initiative and by the agency of the Word.

Just as the first unit of the Prologue introduced information that will figure prominently in the unfolding story, so this second section introduces important concepts and terms that will appear at crucial stages of the narrative. Two examples should suffice to illustrate. First, the audience is told in three separate instances that "the world" hates Jesus and his followers (see 7:1–7; 15:18–21; 17:14–15). These statements should not surprise the reader, who has already been prepared for this rejection by the information provided in vv. 10–11. Second, the concept of rebirth will reappear in Jesus' conversation with Nicodemus in the phrases "born from above" and "born of water and Spirit" (John 3:3, 5). The reader's prior exposure to this metaphor will only serve to heighten an awareness of Nicodemus's seeming inability to understand even the most transparent metaphor used by Jesus.

18. Some scholars think the reference to believing in "his name" here is a reference to the name "Jesus," but I think something far greater is intended here. The connection between the *Logos* and God was explicitly spelled out in 1:1c and is a major theme throughout the gospel. At every turn the Johannine Jesus is emphasizing his organic connection to the Father. As the revealer of all that God is, Jesus has been given the very name of the Father—"I AM." Therefore, I am persuaded that "name" in this context is intended as a reference to the divine name, YHWH. Understanding v. 12 in this way invests this section with greater christological significance.

John 1:14–18: The Word Becomes the Incarnate Son

> 14 And the Word became flesh and tabernacled among us, and we have seen his glory, the glory as of a father's only son, full of grace and truth. 15 (John testified to him and cried out, "This was he of whom I said, 'He who comes after me ranks ahead of me because he was before me.'") 16 From his fullness we have all received, grace upon grace. 17 The law indeed was given through Moses; grace and truth came through Jesus Christ. 18 No one has ever seen God. It is God the only Son, who is close to the Father's heart, who has made him known. (NRSV)

Verse 14 represents the climactic moment in the Prologue in that it depicts the Word *becoming*. To this point the Word has been described in terms of his *eternal existence*; the narrator has accomplished this by using the Greek verb *eimi* ("to be"). The eternal existence of the Word is clearly seen in 1:1–2: "In the beginning *was* (*ēn*) the Word, and the Word *was* (*ēn*) with God, and the Word *was* (*ēn*) God. He *was* (*ēn*) with God in the beginning." In v. 14, the narrator sets up an intentional contrast between what the Word has always been (*eimi*) and what the word has now *become* (Greek: *ginomai*). Never before has the Word *become* something. The Word has always simply *been*. But now, the Word has *become* flesh and has made a home among humanity. The intentional contrast created by the use of verbs for "to be" and "to become" underscores the significance of this incarnation. The Word has been transformed into a new mode of existence on behalf of his people. In this way, the story of Jesus told by the Gospel of John is quite different from what we see in the other NT Gospels. For John, Jesus has quite literally stepped out of the heavens in order to take on human flesh.[19]

Verse 14 contains two other Greek words that call for clarification. First, the affirmation that the Word became flesh and *lived* (Greek: *eskēnōsen*) among humanity expands the basic image of taking on human flesh. The noun *skēnē* ("tent" or "shelter") and the related verb *skēnoō* ("to take up residence") are used in the Septuagint in reference to the tabernacles constructed by the Israelites during their wilderness experience (see Lev 23:42–43). By the time of Jesus, one of the major festal celebrations for the Jewish people was *Sukkoth*, known in the Hebrew Bible as the "Festival of Ingathering" (Exod 23:16; 34:22) or "Festival of the Seventh Month" (Neh 8:14), though it is often known today as the Feast of Tabernacles (see table 2.5). This festival commemorated YHWH's presence with his people while they lived in temporary shelters during their arduous journey through the wilderness. There can be little doubt that this verb is meant to recall the events of the Exodus. We have already indicated that John's Gospel situates the story of Jesus in the wider story of Israel's God as told in Genesis and Exodus. This verse represents one more connection to early stages in YHWH's dealings with Israel. There can also be little doubt that John's Gospel intentionally connects Jesus with the major religious feasts of Israel. This subtle cue in v. 14 is initial evidence of what will become a more prominent theme throughout the

19. The presentation of Jesus "stepping out of the heavens" may have a connection to Isa 64:1–2: "O that you would tear open the heavens and come down, so that the mountains would quake at your presence—as when fire kindles brushwood and the fire causes water to boil—to make your name known to your adversaries, so that the nations might tremble at your presence" (NRSV).

gospel—Jesus as a fulfilment of or replacement for the outward trappings of Jewish religious life.

The second Greek word that begs for clarification is the term *monogenos*—a word that has for centuries been rendered "only begotten." In the Western world this odd phrase has entered the popular consciousness through public recitations of John 3:16, perhaps the most well-known verse in the NT by those within and outside of the Christian tradition. However, this familiar translation is probably rooted in an incorrect understanding of the word's etymology. Previously it was thought that *monogenos* was a compound word comprised of *monos* ("only") and *gennaō* ("to beget" or "to give birth"). Hence, it has been commonplace to speak of Jesus as God's "only begotten son." However, more recent research suggests that the term is a combination of *monos* ("only") and *genos* ("type" or "kind"). This would seem to indicate that, for John, Jesus is "one of a kind" or more appropriately, the "unique one from the Father" rather than the "only begotten of the Father." While it may be true that in the Gospel of John, Jesus *is* the "only begotten" son of God, the term *monogenos* does not point to that truth. Instead, *monogenos* points to the uniqueness of Jesus. He is the only one who has ever existed eternally with God and also the only one to step out of the heavens to take on human flesh. In these ways and others that will emerge throughout the story, Jesus is the "unique one from the Father." Further, the unique one is "full of grace and truth," a phrase that is almost universally regarded as an echo of God's covenant faithfulness toward Israel in Exod 34:6.[20]

The next verse provides the reader with a literary technique known as a "prolepsis." A proleptic statement

20. Exod 34:6: The Lord passed before him, and proclaimed, "The Lord, the Lord, a God merciful and gracious, slow to anger, and *abounding in steadfast love and faithfulness*" (NRSV).

anticipates something that will take place in the narrative and often does so by speaking of that event in the past tense. Verse 15 recounts John's testimony that Jesus is greater than him because of his heavenly origins. This testimony has not yet taken place but will appear almost verbatim in 1:30, on the second day of recorded activity in the narrative. Prolepses are reader-elevating devices that put the reader in a position of privilege and lay the groundwork for something that will happen at a later stage in the narrative. This is one of several instances in which the narrator speaks of an event prior to its occurrence.[21] Once again, John the Baptist appears as the reliable witness commissioned by God to testify on behalf of Jesus.

The incarnation of the Word is a cosmic event that brings about an all-surpassing gift to humanity. In v. 16 this gift is described as the provision of "grace upon grace." The word "grace" (Greek: *charis*) figures prominently in this unit of the Prologue, appearing four times in vv. 14–17. In keeping with our reading strategy of "letting John be John" apart from other first-century interpreters of Jesus, it is necessary to point out that the word "grace" does not mean the same thing here as it does in the writings of Paul.[22] The word more properly refers to a "gift" or "favorable disposition," and it seems clear that God's gift to humanity is Jesus, the Word-made-flesh, who brings light and life to the world. His coming has yielded gift after gift (or an attitude of extreme favor toward humanity).

Verse 17 offers yet another link to Exodus imagery. Moses, the leader who spoke with YHWH face-to-face,

21. One of the more noteworthy examples of a proleptic statement appears in 11:2, where Mary's action of anointing Jesus' feet is mentioned one entire chapter before it actually takes place (see 12:1–8).

22. The term *charis* is ubiquitous in the writings of Paul, and it often refers to the means by which God offers forgiveness of human sin.

was also the great lawgiver who unveiled the Torah to Israel (see Exod 19–20; 34). In the same way, Jesus is the one who has eternally existed face-to-face with God.[23] He alone has unveiled grace and truth which extends God's program begun in Moses. In a final affirmation of the intimate union between Father and Son, the narrator asserts that Jesus is "in the bosom of the father" (v. 18b)—a phrase that will reappear in the scene of Jesus' final meal on the night of his betrayal. As the son who possesses that unique relationship to God, Jesus is the one who reveals the Father to humanity (v. 18c); this is his most important role in the world.

As in the two previous sections of the Prologue, themes are introduced in vv. 14–18 which come into play later in the story. One example is found in ch. 14, where Jesus is discussing with the disciples his imminent departure to the Father. After he insists that no one can come to the Father apart from him (v. 6), Philip proclaims, "Lord, show us the Father and that will be enough for us" (v. 8). The reader already knows that Jesus is one who reveals the Father to humanity (cf. 1:18) and sees this request for what it is—a fundamental misunderstanding of Jesus' origins and identity. Jesus goes on to explain, "Anyone who has seen me has seen the Father" (v. 9)—an explicit affirmation of the statement in 1:18. The reader knows this, but Philip and the other disciples show through their behavior they do not.

READING JOHN IN LIGHT OF THE PROLOGUE

To this point in the chapter we have identified only a handful of instances in which themes from the Prologue recur in the story. Many more examples could be brought forward

23. The phrase translated "with God" (Greek: *pros ton theon*) in 1:1, 2 is used in the sense of a face-to-face interaction. Some scholars prefer to translate it "the Word was face-to-face with God."

but space limitations preclude us from doing so. By way of overview, we have seen that the Word was with God in a unique eternal existence (v. 1–2). The Word was the agent of all creation (v. 3), the light of humanity that enlightens those in the world (vv. 4, 9), and the one with authority to appoint God's children (v. 12). The Word-made-flesh is known as Jesus Christ (vv. 14, 17). He displays God's glory (v. 14), dispenses grace and truth (vv. 16–17), dwells in intimate union with the Father (v. 18b), and reveals the Father to humanity (v. 18c).

Armed with this information, the reader is now in a position to approach the story from an informed perspective. This does not mean that all mystery has been alleviated. Rather, the Prologue lays a foundation for an informed reading of the story but also helps to create a tension that begs for resolution. In this way, the Gospel of John develops understanding in the reader with the promise that even greater understanding will come about at the conclusion of the story. Returning to the illustration with which we began the chapter, the viewer of *Columbo* continues to learn significant things throughout the episode even though s/he has begun with more knowledge than those in the story. When we read the Gospel of John in this way we follow what we have learned down a winding path to new insights we have not known. The stated purpose of the gospel is to engender belief in those who hear the story: "These things have been written in order that you might believe . . . and that believing, you might have life in his name" (20:31). When read in this way, the gospel intends to take its readers on a journey from knowledge (1:1–18) to belief (20:30–31).

KEY CONCEPTS TO KEEP IN MIND WHILE YOU READ:

(1) Jesus has eternal origins (1:1ab)

(2) Jesus possesses all that the Father possesses (1:1c)

(3) Jesus is from above (1:2)

(4) Jesus is the agent of all creation (1:3)

(5) Jesus is the giver of life (1:4)

(6) Jesus is the true light which enlightens all people (1:4–5, 9)

(7) Jesus has come into a world he helped to create and was rejected by his people (1:10–11)

(8) Jesus has the authority to grant eternal life and new birth (1:12–13)

(9) Jesus took on human flesh and became like humans (1:14)

(10) Jesus is the purveyor of grace and brings to completion the economy that existed under Moses (1:17)

(11) Jesus is the one who reveals the Father to humanity (1:18)

KEY TERMS TO KEEP IN MIND WHILE YOU READ:

(1) life (*zōē*) (1:4)

(2) light (*phōs*) (1:4, 5, 7, 8, 9)

(3) darkness (*skotos/skotia*) (1:5)

(4) sent (*apostellō/pempō*) (1:6)

(5) witness (*martyria/martyreō*) (1:7, 8, 15)

(6) the world (*kosmos*) (1:9, 10)

(7) truth/true (*alētheia/alēthinos*) (1:9, 14, 17)

(8) to believe (*pisteuō*) (1:7, 12)

(9) glory (*doxa*) (1:14)

(10) "in the bosom" (*eis ton kolpon*) (1:18)

REFLECTION:

1. How does viewing the Prologue as the "interpretive lens" for the entire story shape or change your approach to reading the Gospel of John?

2. In the chapter we argued that the narrator intends to draw connections between Jesus and the early history of Israel as recounted in Genesis and Exodus. In what ways does this emphasis help you better understand the Christology of the Gospel of John?

Chapter 3

A TALE OF TWO STORIES

JOHN'S TWO-LEVEL DRAMA

IN THE SUMMER OF 2010 my wife and I took our three children (at the time, aged 10, 8, and 5) to the movie theater to see *Toy Story 3*. Given the differences in their ages, it can be difficult to find a movie all three will want to see, but this was a rare exception. Honestly, the two of us were probably as excited as our children to see the final chapter in the story of Andy and his toys. We had been exposed to the first two movies around 2001 and had fallen in love with the story and its characters. Over the first decade of our parenting career we had watched both films numerous times with each of our children. That day, as a family of five we sat anxiously in the theater, waiting for the film to start. It was probably the first time that each one of us was equally excited to see the same movie—a rarity indeed, if you have watched much programming aimed at the entire family.

The *Toy Story* franchise follows the adventures of Andy and his toys, a mixed bag of animate playthings led by Woody, the grounded cowboy who serves as the *de facto* leader of the bunch, and Buzz Lightyear, the occasionally delusional but always entertaining space ranger. The first two movies provide snapshots into different stages of Andy's adolescence and reckon with the ever-present reality that one day he will grow up and no longer need his toys. As the third film begins, Andy is a fully grown teenager preparing to leave for college; the entire movie is driven by the anticipation of Andy's departure into the adventures of young adulthood.

Toward the end of the movie there is a scene in which Andy's mother walks into his empty room and releases an audible gasp. She looks around at the walls that had once been plastered with crayon drawings and Buzz Lightyear posters to see few remnants of her son's waning childhood. She stands face-to-face with the realization that her little boy is no longer little. I am not ashamed to say that at this point in the film my eyes were wet with tears. I had followed Andy's journey from childhood to young adulthood and now I was saying goodbye to him, his room, his toys, his childhood, his innocence. But I was really emotional for another reason. As I sat beside my oldest son, Christopher, I realized that I was not just watching the culmination of the story of Andy and his toys; I was witnessing the story of my own journey. As a young parent I had watched my son live vicariously through Andy's experience. I watched him play with his own toys and wonder if they came alive whenever we left the house. That very year we had begun to experience, firsthand, the waning of *his* adolescence as he lost his final baby tooth, jettisoned his belief in Santa Claus and the Tooth Fairy, and began asking for electronics rather than action figures for his birthday. I cried because I knew that all too soon, I would be standing in a similarly empty room preparing to take *my* son off to college. I looked over at my wife and I knew she was thinking the same thing as tears also filled her eyes. For the both of us, *Toy Story 3* was operating at two levels. At one level we were watching the story of Andy and his toys, while at a deeper, more visceral level, we saw a reflection of our own parental journey in Andy's transition to adulthood and independence.

Some of the biggest blockbuster movies of the past two decades reflect this sort of two-level dynamic, but in a more intentional way. For instance, I cannot think of *Titanic*'s Rose (played by Kate Winslet) without remembering how her character continually betrays the trappings of postmodern thinking in a story world that is historically situated within modernity. After all, what greater testament was there to the ethos of modernity than the launch of the Titanic, the so-called "unsinkable" ship? But Rose seems to move through the world of 1912 with a complex, postmodern worldview that comes straight out of 1997. Or consider the blockbuster film *Braveheart*, where Mel Gibson's William Wallace fights for a "freedom" that looks very much like the twentieth-century American dream and shares precious little with the worldview held by Scots at the turn of the fourteenth century. With films in particular, historical stories must be grounded in a realistic socio-historical context if they are to be regarded as authentic, but must also contain some key element that will resonate with the intended modern audience. This is what I refer to as "the Hollywood effect" and I like to tell my students that it is also at work in the Gospel of John.

Scholars have long recognized that the Gospel of John is a two-level drama, operating similarly to what I have described above. At its most basic level, John's Gospel recounts one version of Jesus' origins, life, vocation, and death, while beneath the surface is a story of the community for whom the gospel was originally written. To say it differently, the Gospel of John tells the story of Jesus while also revealing the story of a community in crisis. Before we can examine what this means for our reading of the Gospel of John, we first need to consider several different viewpoints that have exercised considerable influence over this discussion.

STAGES OF GOSPEL DEVELOPMENT

With the rise of form criticism in the early twentieth century, NT scholars began to place a great deal of emphasis on reconstructing the *world behind the text* (for more on form criticism, see the brief discussion in table 2.4 above). In other words, the form critics were concerned with discovering how the text came to exist in its final form, though they were not always particularly interested in *interpreting* the text in its final form. Because of this emphasis, form critics expended tremendous energy in trying to distinguish material arising out of the life setting of Jesus from traditions that developed in the life setting of the early Church.[1] As noted in the previous chapter, the form critics thought that it was possible to isolate certain traditions in the gospels and assign them to different stages in the life of the early church. This way of thinking ultimately led to a widely accepted view that saw three stages of tradition in the gospels:

Stage 1: Traditions from the Ministry of Jesus—material arising from the teaching and vocational activity of Jesus in the late 20s CE.

Stage 2: The Post-Resurrection Preaching of Jesus' Disciples—religious convictions that developed about Jesus in the first few decades after his death (ca. 30 to 50 CE).

Stage 3: The Writing of the Gospels by the Four Evangelists—texts and traditions about Jesus that developed during the writing of the gospel narratives (between

1. Since most of this research was arising out of the German academy, much of the language used by scholars reflects this. Within New Testament research, these two life settings are referred to as the *Sitz im Leben Jesu* (the life setting of Jesus) and *Sitz im Leben der Kirche* (the life setting of church), respectively.

70 and 95 CE); what is often referred to as the "life setting of the church."[2]

Table 3.1

Expelled from the Synagogue?

In 1968, J. Louis Martyn published *History and Theology in the Fourth Gospel*, a groundbreaking work in which he argued (1) that the primary background of the Gospel of John was Jewish; and (2) that within John's community, a rift developed in the synagogue between Jewish followers of Jesus and observant Jews who did not follow Jesus. This rift, he argued, led to the former group being expelled from the synagogue, and this event is reflected in John 9:22, 12:42, and 16:2. Martyn argued that the Jewish benediction against heretics—the *Birkat ha-Minim*—stood behind this historical situation. He also argued that the statement, "the Jews had already decided that anyone who acknowledged that Jesus was the Messiah would be put out of the synagogue" (9:22) refers to conversations in the academy at Jamnia led by Rabbi Gamaliel II (ca. 80–115 CE), which formulated the benediction. Scholars today are less certain about the role of the *Birkat ha-Minim*, and a number of other details from Martyn's reconstruction have also been questioned or discarded by scholars. Nevertheless, Martyn's work remains foundational for research on the Gospel of John. *History and Theology in the Fourth Gospel* is still widely cited and is now in a third edition.

The quintessential example used to illustrate these three stages is the episode in which Jesus heals the man born blind in John 9. In that passage, Jesus mixes his saliva with

2. This view, which developed in Protestant circles, was ultimately embraced by the Roman Catholic church under Pope Pius XII in his Encyclical on Biblical Studies, *Divino Afflante Spiritu* (1943). This position was reaffirmed by the document *Dei Verbum*, on Divine Revelation, at Vatican II (1963–1965) and subsequent documents, including the Pontifical Biblical Commission's document, "Instruction on the Historical Truth of the Gospels" (§6–9).

dirt to create mud, which he then places upon the young man's eyes, allowing him to see for the first time (9:1–12).[3] After the healing takes place, the young man is questioned by the religious leaders (9:13–17, 24–34), as are his parents (9:18–23), who refuse to testify on his behalf for fear that they will be expelled from the synagogue.

Using this passage as a model, scholars have attempted to locate remnants of all three stages of gospel development. With respect to the first stage—traditions from the ministry of Jesus—it is widely accepted that Jesus had a reputation as a healer during his lifetime. The entirety of John 9 assumes that Jesus has the ability to heal, and scholars believe this bedrock assumption finds its basis in the historical ministry of Jesus.

Many casual readers of the Bible assume that everything they read in the New Testament reflects "what actually happened," but it is not always that simple. In fact, such a view is rather naïve in light of how difficult it can be to isolate historical material in the gospels with any real precision. Generally speaking, scholars find it easier to detect traditions and beliefs that developed in the decades after Jesus' death. For example, many scholars think it unlikely that anyone regarded Jesus as divine during his lifetime. Within the context of strict monotheistic Judaism, this idea would have been considered blasphemous. Instead, this conviction developed over time and became an essential belief in

3. This particular sign miracle provides the reader with a new revelation about Jesus. Up to this point in the story he has healed contracted illnesses (see John 4:46–54; 5:1–8) but he has not yet been faced with a congenital issue. By healing the man born blind, Jesus demonstrates his power over both contracted and congenital illnesses. The seven "signs" in the Gospel of John progress in their scope and intensity. In ch. 11, Jesus performs his final "sign" in raising Lazarus from the dead. Raising Lazarus not only demonstrates his power over death, but also anticipates his own resurrection.

the years immediately after Jesus' death. As we discussed in the previous chapter, the divinity of Jesus became *the* foundational christological view for the early church, and that continues to be the case up to the present day. Against this backdrop, when we read John 9 and see that the healed man not only refers to Jesus as "Lord" (Greek: *kyrios*), but also begins to worship him (see v. 38), we must realize that we are most likely dealing with a tradition that developed in the early decades after Jesus' death. In other words, we are not reading something that took place during the ministry of Jesus. Instead, we have an example of a theological truth which Jesus' early followers "discovered" about him in their process of theological reflection, and subsequently introduced into the narrative. The form critics argue that this element of the story represents material from the second stage of gospel development—convictions about Jesus that developed among his earliest disciples. We will say more about this below, but for now it is important to point out that while the "three stages" model is not perfect, it provides us with some helpful categories in our thinking about the development of the four gospels.

Attempts to locate traditions from the third stage of development have perhaps been the most controversial in recent years. After the young man is healed in John 9, his parents are called to testify on his behalf. Though they are certain that this is their son, they refuse to speak for fear that they will be "put out of the synagogue" (9:22). Over the past several decades, much has been made of the phrase "be put out of the synagogue" (Greek: *aposynagōgos genētai*, 9:22; 12:42; 16:2), which occurs nowhere else in the New Testament. Recent scholarship has accepted that the phrase "to be put out of the synagogue" represents a historical reality faced by the author of the gospel and his community. The scholar most closely associated with this view is J. Louis

Martyn. At the heart of Martyn's argument lies the assumption that a split occurred in the Christian community to which the Gospel of John was written. Part of this split included a group of Jesus followers being expelled from the synagogue on the basis of their belief in Jesus as Messiah. Martyn's reconstruction was brilliantly articulated and brought about a sea change in scholarship on the Gospel

TABLE 3.2

Was the Gospel of John Written for *All* Christians?

In 1998, Richard Bauckham published an edited volume entitled, *The Gospels for All Christians: Rethinking the Gospel Audiences*. His introductory essay, "For Whom Were the Gospels Written?" (9–48), argued that the notion of gospel communities was rooted in a speculation that was unwarranted. Recognizing the early and widespread circulation of the four gospels, Bauckham argued that we should dispense with the idea of "Gospel communities" and explore the idea that the gospels were originally composed for a universal Christian audience. The book was heralded by some as the harbinger of a new era in NT studies. Fifteen years later, Bauckham's theory has not been met with widespread acceptance, though it has spawned interesting and fruitful conversations. Among those who were quick to embrace the theory were scholars with strong commitments to the historicity of the New Testament. Those scholars remain the most vocal advocates of Bauckham's thesis.

In 2010, Bauckham's former student, Edward Klink, published a volume devoted to examining the impact of Bauckham's thesis. The book, *The Audience of the Gospels: The Origin and Function of the Gospels in Early Christianity*, included contributions from scholars who were both sympathetic and unsympathetic to Bauckham's original thesis. See also Klink, *The Sheep of the Fold: The Audience and Origin of the Gospel of John*; Klink, "The Gospel Community Debate: State of the Question."

of John. While many today have questioned some of the details of Martyn's theory, the basic assumption of a two-level drama remains the dominant position. Martyn's view is discussed in greater detail above (see table 3.1). For now, we need to recognize that we are once again faced with an element in the story that is out of keeping with what was taking place in Jesus' historical situation.

The movement that grew out of devotion to Jesus was not large enough during his lifetime for such a critical divide to have developed among worshippers in the synagogue. However, in the decades after his death, devotion to Jesus had grown to such proportions that a division of this kind could have developed. The official "parting of the ways" between Judaism and Christianity was still in the distant future and it seems clear that followers of Jesus continued worshipping in the synagogue well into the second century.[4] To say all of this more plainly, in John 9 we are faced with a historical disagreement in which the story of *John's community* is being read back into the story of Jesus' life. Such historical disagreements are called "anachronisms"—elements of a given story that are out of place with the historical context of the story itself. When illustrating this feature of the narrative with my students, I find it helpful to discuss the prevalence of historical mistakes in modern movies.

The Academy Award-winning film *Forrest Gump* is known for its numerous historical blunders; two in particular stand out for our purposes. First, during a scene which is set in 1970, Forrest (played by Tom Hanks) is perusing a copy of the newspaper *USA Today*. Since the paper did not

4. What we may see in the Johannine community is a local "parting of the ways" that reflects a fairly significant divide between Jews in the synagogue and a mixed community (Jewish and Gentile) that expressed devotion to Jesus.

begin its official circulation until 1982, this scene is problematic historically. While the details are not in keeping with what we know to be historically accurate, this inaccuracy does not detract from the overall realism or artistic value of the scene. To say it another way, the anachronism is a problem for the historian but not for the viewer. A second anachronism appears while Forrest unsuccessfully attempts to catch shrimp for the first time. Pulling his supposed catch onto the boat, Forrest empties the net only to find that he has trudged up a bunch of junk from the bottom of the sea. Among the junk he hauls aboard is an empty can of Mello Yello. Forrest's shrimping adventures are supposedly taking place in the early 1970s, just after his return from the Vietnam War, but Mello Yello was not introduced to the public until March of 1979. Again, this scene contradicts history but does not detract from the artistic value or realism of the scene; the discrepancy only becomes problematic for those viewers who are concerned with historical precision.[5]

Another example that I use with my students—and one that I think captures the essence of this particular scene in the Gospel of John more robustly—considers the legacy of the American civil rights movement in the late 1950s and early 1960s. If, while recounting the story of the "March on Washington," I were to place Barack Obama arm-in-arm

5. In his book *The Historical Christ and the Theological Jesus*, Dale Allison discusses a rather famous example of historical anachronism which is found in the John Keats sonnet, "On First Looking into Chapman's Homer." The sonnet closes with these words: "Then felt I like some watcher of the skies, When a new planet swims into his ken; Or like stout Cortez when with eagle eyes, He star'd at the Pacific—and all his men Look'd at each other with a wild surmise—silent, upon a peak in Darien." History tells us that it was Balboa and not Cortez who discovered the Pacific Ocean, though this is of little consequence for the literary value of the sonnet. Allison goes on to quote the literary scholar M. H. Abrams, who wrote that the factual mistake "matters to history but not to poetry" (33).

with Martin Luther King Jr., A. Philip Randolph, Roy Wilkins, Whitney Young, and other prominent figures in the civil rights movement, anyone remotely familiar with the historical event would immediately object that Obama was not present. A little bit of historical investigation would further reveal that he was only two years and twenty-four days old and living in Hawaii when the event took place on August 28, 1963. However, for Americans who are cognizant of the import and legacy of the civil rights movement, there can be little doubt that Barack Obama's presidency is critically linked to the events of that day. In his well-known "I Have a Dream" speech, Dr. Martin Luther King Jr. openly longed for a world in which people would be judged not by the color of their skin but by the content of their character. The election of Barack Obama—America's first African American president—must surely be regarded as at least a partial fulfillment of Dr. King's hope for the future. By placing Obama arm-in-arm with the great civil rights leaders, I speak to my contemporary audience about past events and their significance for the present; this example is useful for us in understanding the kind of anachronism we encounter in John 9. While it is unlikely that following Jesus caused individuals to be excommunicated from the synagogue during Jesus' lifetime, it does seem certain this was happening during the latter part of the first century when the gospel was written. By situating this later event in the story of Jesus' life and ministry, John speaks to his contemporary audience about past events and their importance for the present. As the one who reveals the Father to humanity, Jesus confronts the world with a choice that necessarily causes division. One must either accept or reject the identity of the Johannine Jesus (cf. 1:12–13), and to do either is to risk division in the critical spheres of one's life.

Material in the gospels rarely breaks down as neatly as what has been suggested above. For my part, I am not fully convinced that all three stages of gospel development are present in John 9 in precisely the way they have been articulated. For our purposes in this book, we will focus on two interwoven stories—the story of Jesus and the story of John's community. It is therefore important for us to recognize that the Gospel of John reveals clues which suggest that it was written for a specific community that needed reminding of the ongoing significance of identifying with Jesus. Before we can do this, however, we need to take a closer look at the Johannine community.

THE COMMUNITY OF JOHN?

The above discussion hinges upon the existence of a "Johannine community," a construct which is admittedly based on scholarly speculation. For decades it was accepted that the gospels were written for specific communities, though this idea has come under some scrutiny in recent years. Promoting a thesis that has received a great deal of attention—both positive and negative—Richard Bauckham has argued quite forcefully that the gospels were originally intended for all Christians and that the idea of gospel communities needs to be jettisoned (see table 3.2). There is not space here to discuss all of the arguments leveled against the idea that the gospels were originally written for individual communities. We are concerned here with the evidence for a community associated with the Gospel of John, and must ask if such an idea is still viable. In other words, was there a community of John and what, if anything, can we know about it?

First, it is critical to note that unlike the Synoptic Gospels, our knowledge of John's community is aided by the presence of three epistles bearing John's name (1, 2, 3

John). These letters are written in the same style and with much of the same vocabulary as the gospel, and there is widespread agreement among scholars that the gospel and letters arose from within the same context. This means that a reconstruction of a Johannine community rests on a much more secure foundation than do the other theoretical gospel communities. In short, we have fairly specific knowledge that a Johannine community existed. We are not able to reconstruct its history with the same rigor and precision as previous scholars have attempted. But we have, at the very least, evidence of a community, near the end of the first century, struggling to come to terms with what it means to follow Jesus.

Second, it is fallacious to assume that a document written for a specific community cannot also speak to other, broader contexts. This is one mistake commonly made by advocates of a "Gospel-for-all-Christians" theory. There is no question that the Gospel of John circulated widely at an early date, but this should not be taken as evidence that it was originally intended for a universal Christian audience. Let's consider another example: the first known commentaries on the Gospel of John were written by the Valentinian Gnostics, Ptolemy and Heracleon.[6] History also tells us that the Gnostics favored the Gospel of John and regarded it as authoritative. Should we then take this to mean that John's Gospel was originally intended for a wide circulation among various Gnostic sects?[7] The reasoning falls apart here. It is conceivable—and in fact preferable to

6. Sometime between 140 and 160, Ptolemy composed a commentary on a portion of John's Prologue (1:1–14), while Heracleon (ca. 170 CE) wrote a commentary on the entire gospel.

7. This same type of reasoning is often applied, erroneously, to the *Gospel of Thomas*—which many think is Gnostic because it was used widely by later Gnostic groups.

argue—that the Gospel of John could have been written for a specific community and that subsequently, other groups also found it to be authoritative for faith and practice.[8]

Third, arguments raised by those who reject a two-level reading often reveal an overly optimistic belief in or rigid commitment to the historicity of the Gospel of John (i.e., the viewpoint that everything in the gospel is "historical"). As noted previously, many devotional readers of the Bible struggle to come to terms with the idea that not everything in the New Testament happened exactly as it is narrated; consequently, one of several responses ensues. Those on one extreme decide to reject the idea and continue to insist on the historicity of the entire New Testament. Some on the opposite end of the spectrum follow historical uncertainties down a path that leads them to reject everything in the New Testament as questionable or unhistorical. However, each of these responses is an illegitimate and intellectually dishonest response to what we find in the New Testament. There is another way to approach these issues, but it requires an abandonment of the quest for certainty. In order to read the Gospel of John faithfully, we must approach it with an awareness of how religious writings functioned in the ancient world. If we impose our modern sensibilities on the text we are making an illegitimate move, and if we insist that the text must conform to our modern theological constructs, we are making an equally illegitimate move. The Gospel of John is a theologically stylized narrative with historical roots, which most closely resembles Greco-Roman biography (*bios*).

As I stated in chapter 1, one of my goals is to help those who use this book become better and more perceptive readers of the Gospel of John. Such a process demands

8. For an argument that supports this line of thinking, see Blomberg, "Gospels for Specific Communities *and* All Christians," 111–33.

intellectual honesty and requires that one's presuppositions will occasionally be challenged and even discarded. A rigid commitment to the historicity of the Gospel of John precludes such honesty at the outset, and necessarily short-circuits the process of becoming a more perceptive reader of the text. By the same token, a rejection of all history in the gospel is equally dangerous. Story, history, and theology need to be held in a necessary tension, and that will allow us to appreciate the voices at work within the narrative. As we move forward, our reading of the Gospel of John will operate under the assumption that the narrative tells the story of Jesus while unveiling the concerns of a specific community in the late first century. We will also consider how the text speaks to our contemporary settings.

REFLECTION:

1. How does knowing that the Gospel of John was written for a specific community impact your reading experience?

2. In what ways can an understanding of John's two-level drama help you understand the gospel's message for a contemporary audience? How might an appreciation for this two-level drama assist you in understanding what is being communicated to the world *in front of the text*?

Chapter 4

JOHN, JESUS, AND JUDAISM

IS THE GOSPEL OF JOHN JEWISH AND ANTI-JEWISH AT THE SAME TIME?

(OR, IS THE GOSPEL OF JOHN SCHIZOPHRENIC?)[1]

In 2001, while playing point guard for the New York Knicks, Charlie Ward made several disparaging and widely publicized remarks about Jews in a team Bible study. Ward, a former two-sport athlete at Florida State University, is perhaps best known for winning the 1993 Heisman Trophy—the highest honor given to a college football player in the United States. While discussing Jesus' persecution and death, Ward reportedly said: "Jews are stubborn . . . tell

1. I am especially indebted to Frank Moloney for his careful reading and insightful critique of the weaknesses in an earlier draft of this chapter. Though I am no longer formally his student, he continues to teach me.

me, why did they persecute Jesus unless he knew something they didn't want to accept? . . . They had his blood on their hands."[2] When he was later asked to provide context for his comments, Ward responded: "If you want to know what the context is, go to the Bible."[3] As you can imagine, these comments did not play well in New York City, which boasts the second largest population of ethnically Jewish residents in the world.[4] Ward insisted that he would never disparage Jews because, "my best friend is a Jewish guy, and his name is Jesus Christ."[5] Nevertheless, in the first game after his statements were made, Ward was booed relentlessly by his home fans, and later chastised in a strongly worded statement by then NBA commissioner, David Stern, himself a Jewish man.

Sadly, the bald and unqualified assertion "The Jews killed Jesus" is shared by many people, including serious readers of the New Testament. A poll conducted by the Anti-Defamation League in October 2013 found that roughly 26 percent of Americans believe that Jews were responsible for the death of Jesus, down only slightly from 31 percent of those polled in 2011. Contemporary Christians have given this idea little thought, and the result is that Jewish culpability for Jesus' death has been perpetuated in popular preaching, publications, and presentations of Jesus' life.[6]

2. "Comments by 2 Knicks Called Anti-Semitic," *New York Times*, April 21, 2001.

3. "Ward Refers Writers to Bible," *New York Times*, April 22, 2001.

4. New York City has the second largest population of Jewish residents at around 2 million. This amounts to approximately 15% of the world's Jewish population. With this population, New York is second only to Tel Aviv, the capital city of the state of Israel.

5. "Comments by 2 Knicks Called Anti-Semitic," *New York Times*, April 21, 2001.

6. A particularly clear example of this phenomenon can be seen in the blockbuster movie, *Passion of the Christ*. Notorious for his public displays of anti-Semitic behavior, director Mel Gibson made

Table 4.1

Judaism(s) in the First Century: The Case for Complexity

Many modern Christians assume that there was one monolithic form of Judaism during the lifetime of Jesus. Students will often ask, "What was the Jewish view of X during the time of Jesus?" I often respond that this is like asking, "What is the Christian view of baptism?" or "How do Christians conceive of the Eucharist?" These questions require very complex answers though they are too often framed in such a way as to suggest that there is only one answer. During the first century there were numerous sects within Judaism, many of which we meet in the New Testament. Among these groups were the Pharisees, Sadduccees, Essenes, Zealots, *Sicarii*, and Herodians. For a robust discussion of sectarian Judaism during this period, see Shaye J. D. Cohen, *From the Maccabees to the Mishnah*, 3rd ed., chap. 5.

Much of this thinking is rooted in a history of lamentable anti-Jewish sentiment fostered by Christians—a sentiment that extends to some of the earliest Christian writings. For example, in his well-known homily *Peri Pascha* ("On the Passover"), Melito of Sardis, writing in 167 CE, provides the earliest recorded charge of "deicide," or the killing of God. In an extended section of the sermon, Melito writes:

> And where has he been murdered? In the middle of Jerusalem. By whom? By Israel? . . . What

Jewish culpability for Jesus' death a key element in his film. By and large, Romans are depicted as compassionate toward Jesus while the Jews in the story appear bloodthirsty and bent on destroying Jesus. In one scene that derives from Jesus' trial in the Gospel of Matthew, Pilate is about to release Jesus when the Jewish crowds shout, "Let his blood be upon us and our children!" (Matt 27:25). When asked to remove these words from the film, Gibson obliged but only partially; he removed the English subtitles while retaining the words of the crowds in Aramaic. Only those with knowledge of Aramaic would have caught this.

> strange crime, Israel, have you committed? You dishonoured him that honoured you; you denied him that acknowledged you; you disclaimed him that proclaimed you; you killed him that made you live. . . . The Lord is insulted, *God has been murdered*, the King of Israel has been destroyed by the right hand of Israel.[7]

This sort of anti-Jewish thinking continued to grow in the early centuries of the Church and reached its apex in the Christian writings of the medieval period; such thinking continues to be a problem among contemporary Christians, many of whom feel that this idea emerges simply from a plain reading of the New Testament (on the mistaken notion of a "plain reading," see Starting Point 5 in chapter 1).

Nowhere is Jewish opposition to Jesus seemingly more obvious than in the Gospel of John, in which the narrator relentlessly grinds an axe against a group known as "the Jews" (Greek: *hoi Ioudaioi*). On the surface, the relationship of the Gospel of John to Judaism can be puzzling; two issues in particular contribute to this potential confusion. First, most contemporary scholars hold that the gospel derives from a Jewish background, as evidenced by its emphasis on important Jewish ideas, traditions, and theological motifs. A second and more problematic concern is the gospel's consistent use of the phrase "the Jews" to denote the enemies of Jesus. A superficial reading of the gospel would seem to indicate that John is both sympathetic and antagonistic toward Judaism at the same time. Wayne Meeks has perceptively stated the problem in this way: "To put the matter sharply, with some risk of misunderstanding, the Fourth Gospel is the most anti-Jewish just at the points it is most Jewish."[8] This chapter will attempt both to shed some light on these concerns and get to

7. Melito of Sardis, *Peri Pascha*, 70–96, emphasis added.

8. Meeks, "Am I a Jew?," 172.

the bottom of the tension between John's Jewish background and apparent polemic against "the Jews."

THE JEWISH BACKGROUND OF THE GOSPEL OF JOHN

The background of John's Gospel has been a topic of seemingly endless speculation among scholars. For decades it was assumed that John's dualistic language (light/dark, truth/lie, from above/from below, etc.) and the *Logos* imagery of the Prologue were two indicators that the gospel was borrowing heavily from Greek philosophical ideas. These were, after all, hallmarks of the Greek philosophical tradition dating back several centuries. Others have suggested that the dualistic language was an indication that John was an early Gnostic writing. It was noted in the previous chapter that the two earliest known commentaries on the Gospel of John were written by the Gnostic Christians, Ptolemy (ca. 140–160) and Heracleon (ca. 170 CE)—though this reveals nothing about the gospel's provenance and original audience.[9] Still others have read John's *Logos* in light of rabbinic mysticism, the writings of Philo,[10] and the Qumran corpus.[11] Several recent scholars have even argued that a

9. It is naïve to assume that, just because a particular writing became popular among certain groups, the writing was originally intended for those groups.

10. Philo of Alexandria (also known as Philo Judaeus) was a Jewish philosopher who lived in Alexandria during a period that overlapped with the lives of both Jesus and Paul (ca. 25 BCE–40 CE). The majority of his philosophical writings were either commentaries or extended discourses on the Old Testament. Scholars have found many ideas in John that appear to have a connection with Philo's writings. His impact on Christianity has been lasting insofar as it influenced patristic writers like Clement of Alexandria, Origen, and Ambrose. For more information on Philo, see Danielou, *Philo of Alexandria*.

11. For a series of fresh reflections on John's potential connections

response to Roman imperial ideology played a significant part in shaping the gospel.[12] Despite these proposals, however, it is quite widely acknowledged by scholars today that the Gospel of John situates its story of Jesus squarely within first-century Judaism.[13] Thus, the Prologue, its *Logos* language, and John's unique story of Jesus should all be read and understood in light of the Torah along with first-century expressions of Judaism (for more on this, see the treatment of the Prologue offered in chapter 2). In what follows, we will briefly discuss the Jewish roots of John's Gospel before moving on to the much more complicated issue of "the Jews" in John.

When approaching a complex discussion like the religious thought-world of the Fourth Gospel, everyone would be helped significantly by an abundance of explicit material in the text that would point us in a specific direction. However, readers of John's Gospel do not have the luxury of having access to such material. Instead, we must turn to subtle elements of the story to draw out important motifs and theological emphases. As Adele Reinhartz has astutely noted, nearly all of the elements in the narrative are Jewish, and "because their Jewishness is taken for granted, *it is not emphasized directly in any way*. Nevertheless, Jesus' Jewish context is evident in numerous details."[14] We have already argued at length in chapter 2 that the major themes of the

to the Dead Sea Scrolls, see Coloe and Thatcher, *John, Qumran, and the Dead Sea Scrolls*.

12. See, e.g., Thatcher, *Greater than Caesar*; Carter, *John and Empire*; Richey, *Roman Imperial Ideology and the Gospel of John*. See also my chapter, "John's Gospel and the Roman Imperial Context," in *Jesus Is Lord, Caesar Is Not*, 116–29.

13. For a helpful discussion of the influences on John's religious thought, see Brown, *Introduction to the Gospel of John*, 115–50.

14. Reinhartz, "Judaism in the Gospel of John," 382, emphasis added.

Prologue are transparent in their connections to both Genesis and Exodus. What other elements of the narrative can be brought forward to affirm the Jewishness of the gospel?

First, and most importantly, numerous characters that are not explicitly identified as Jews are, in fact, Jewish: Jesus, his mother, John the Baptist, Lazarus, Martha, Mary, Mary Magdalene, Joseph of Arimathea, and others. Also, most, if not all, of his disciples are Jewish, as evidenced by their Jewish names; two exceptions are Andrew (1:35–40) and Philip (1:43–44), though the presence of a Greek name does not necessarily preclude a Jewish identity. Very often these characters appear in conflict with those explicitly identified as *hoi Ioudaioi*, enabling us to see that *Ioudaios* is not strictly an ethnic designation. Rather, those identified as "the Jews" have made a christological decision to reject Jesus and his message, and thereby reject the One who sent him (see 15:18—16:3). We will discuss this more below.

Second, the physical and situational settings within the story are Jewish. Jesus' ministry takes place in Judea and its environs in the first century CE. Jesus' disciples consistently use the Jewish term "rabbi" when approaching him (1:38, 49; 3:2, 26; 4:31; 6:25; 9:2; 11:8; 20:16), and when he teaches he relies heavily upon texts and themes drawn—both explicitly and implicitly—from the Hebrew Scriptures.[15] It is difficult to deny these patently Jewish features of the narrative, even if they are not expressly emphasized.

Third, the manner in which John constructs his Christology is evidence of a thoroughly Jewish way of thinking. For example, at the outset of his ministry, Jesus is proclaimed to be the "Lamb of God" by John the Baptist

15. An incomplete list of quotations and allusions contains the following: Ps 69:9 is quoted in John 2:17; Num 21:9 is alluded to in John 3:14; Exod 16:4 and Ps 78 are alluded to in John 6:31; Isa 54:13 and Jer 31:33 are alluded to in John 6:45; Num 35:30 is mentioned in John 8:17; Ps 82:6 is directly quoted in John 10:34.

(1:29, 36). This pronouncement serves as a "prolepsis" or an audience-elevating device that points forward to Jesus' death at the end of the story. It seems clear that John intends to present Jesus as the ultimate Passover Lamb.[16] This presentation is assisted by John's changing of the Passion week chronology from what is found in the Synoptic Gospels; in John, Jesus is condemned to die at the very moment lambs are being prepared for sacrifice in the temple.[17] The theological significance of this moment should not be understated. Another element of John's christological presentation is the gospel's insistence on Jesus' connection to the great "I am" of the Hebrew Bible. When the name of God is revealed on Mount Sinai, God announces to Moses, "I am who I am" (see Exod 3:7–15). This name goes on to have tremendous significance within both the Torah and the wider context(s) of Second Temple Judaism. (For further insights into the divine name, see the lengthy discussion of Jesus' "I am" statements in chapter 5.) It is therefore important to note that Jesus' consistent use of "I am" (Greek: *egō eimi*) in reference to himself is evidence of thinking that fits within an explicitly Jewish framework.

Fourth, it has long been recognized that the important days of the Jewish calendar have served as the locus for christologically significant activity in the Gospel of John. Jesus not only engages in important activities on the Sabbath (5:16; 7:22–23; 9:14), but also, one might say *especially*, during the important Jewish feasts (for more on the feasts, see table 2.5 above).[18] It is often the case that the feasts are

16. For more on this, see Skinner, "Another Look at the Lamb of God," 89–104.

17. On this interpretation of the text, see Brown, *Gospel according to John*, 2:556.

18. For further reading on this subject, see Yee, *Jewish Feasts and the Gospel of John*.

reinterpreted in light of Jesus' appearance, so that some scholars argue that Jesus ostensibly replaces the feast or the

TABLE 4.2

Israel's Sacred Year

Hebrew name	*Equivalent in the Gregorian Calendar*	*Feast name*	*Day(s) of the month*
Nisan	March–April	Passover	14
		Unleavened Bread	15–21
		Firstfruits	17
Iyyar	April–May		
Sivan	May–June	Weeks (Pentecost)	7
Tammuz	June–July		
'Ab	July–August	Destruction of the Temple Fast	9
'Elul	August–September		
Tishri	September–October	Trumpets	1
		Day of Atonement	10
		Tabernacles	15–22
Marheshvan	October–November		
Chislev	November–December	Dedication (Hanukkah)	25
Tebeth	December–January		
Shebat	January–February		
'Adar	February–March	Purim	14–15

temple itself. Though there is not space here to evaluate this so-called "replacement" motif, the very nature of the conversation assumes a distinctly Jewish background.

The above represents only a partial list of Jewish features in the narrative, but even when these elements are considered, it seems clear that the Fourth Gospel arose from within a Jewish context. Against that backdrop, and in light of the gospel's consistent emphasis on love, how are we to account for John's apparent hatred for a group known simply as "the Jews?"

WHO ARE "THE JEWS"?

In the Synoptic Gospels readers are introduced to an array of groups within Jewish society—Pharisees, Sadducces, Herodians, chief priests, scribes, elders, tax collectors, and various crowds. While a few of these groups appear in John, the most common term in the gospel for those who interact with and oppose Jesus is the generic designation, "the Jews" (Greek: *hoi Ioudaioi*). This term is used seventy-one times in the Gospel of John compared to sixteen times across all three Synoptic Gospels. To complicate matters further, this group is often hostile toward Jesus and actively seeks both to entrap and kill him. Few issues have received as much attention from interpreters over the past sixty years as the identity of "the Jews" in the Gospel of John. It is also difficult to disentangle this discussion from a broader awareness of Christian anti-Semitism and anti-Judaism that have been so prominent throughout the history of the Church. For many, it seems obvious that John intends to blame the Jews as a representative group for opposing and killing Jesus. But, what seems obvious to many at a surface level actually requires further investigation and a more nuanced explanation. The Gospel of John plays a foundational role in the expressions of contemporary Christian theology, and in a post-Holocaust world where Jewish-Christian dialogue has become critically important to many, this terminology begs for clarification.

What Does *Ioudaios* Mean?

The modern debate over the translation of this word has revolved primarily around two options: "Jew" and "Judean." For centuries, English Bibles have rendered the Greek term

Ioudaios as "Jew" with little or no explanation.[19] This practice continues today. However, some modern English translations have sought to soften this problematic terminology by including a translational gloss like, "the Jewish leaders," though others insist that this practice is taking too much interpretive license.[20] While great attention has been paid to this issue within Biblical scholarship, little of it seems to have filtered down to the way translators treat this particular phrase in John.

Table 4.3

The Significance of Jew v. Judean

The standard Greek lexicon used by students of NT Greek is *A Greek-English Lexicon of the New Testament and Other Early Christian Literature*, 3rd ed. When the 3rd edition appeared in 2000, the editor, Frederick Danker, included a new and helpful comment under the heading for *Ioudaios*, which read:

"Incalculable harm has been caused by simply glossing [*Ioudaios*] with 'Jew', for many readers or auditors of Bible translations do not practice the historical judgment necessary to distinguish between circumstances and events of an ancient time and contemporary ethnic-religious-social realities, with the result that anti-Judaism in the modern sense of the term is needlessly fostered through biblical text" (478).

19. Among popular English translations, see NAB, NRSV, NASB, NKJV, HCSB, NCV, and The Message.

20. The ESV reads, "the Jews," accompanied by a note that reads: "The Greek word *Ioudaioi* refers specifically here to Jewish religious leaders, and others under their influence, who opposed Jesus in that time." The NIV, NET, and CET all read, "the Jewish leaders," and the GNT reads, "the Jewish authorities."

Among those who have argued for a translation other than, "Jew," Steve Mason has been particularly influential. In his works, Mason has consistently rendered *Ioudaios* as "Judean" arguing it captures a more precise meaning of the term in that it better accounts for the complexity we see in Greek sources of that era. *Ioudaios* is used elsewhere to refer to those who belong ethnically to the region of Judea without necessarily commenting on their religious persuasion. Specifically, Mason argues that, even though it is assumed in our modern discussions, there was no such category as "Judaism" in the Greco-Roman world. There was no "religion" understood as "Judaism" and the term *Ioudaioi* was understood, at least until late antiquity, as an ethnic group with its own unique laws, traditions, customs, and deity. Mason also argues that, in addition to being a more accurate rendering, "Judean" is also the more ethical translation since it helps combat the inherent anti-Semitism that has been such a prominent feature of traditional Christianity.[21]

While numerous scholars have followed Mason's lead in translating *Ioudaios* as "Judean," another recent argument has emerged in which scholars are urged to avoid removing Jews from the text altogether. A.-J. Levine, a well-known Jewish New Testament scholar has expressed her concern that removing or replacing the word "Jew" will ultimately lead to a text that is "purified of Jews."[22] She continues: "Complementing this erasure, scholars then proclaim that Jesus is neither Jew nor even Judean, but a Galilean. . . . Once Jesus is not a Jew or a Judean, but a Galilean, it is also an easy step to make him an Aryan. So much

21. These emphases can be found in multiple publications, but the following article is particularly apropos to the discussion of this chapter: Mason, "Jews, Judaeans, Judaizing, Judaism."

22. Levine, *Misunderstood Jew*, 160.

for the elimination of anti-Semitism by means of changing vocabulary."[23]

Both of these arguments raise important points that need to be taken into consideration. Mason recognizes that our use of "Jew" is not only historically inaccurate, but also that it has the potential to engender anti-Semitism. Levine's caution is meant to prevent further anti-Semitic readings of the gospel. A larger question for our purposes—since this book is aimed at non-specialist readers rather than bible translators—is where does this discussion lead us in the goal of becoming better, more perceptive readers of the Gospel of John? First, we must recognize that there is no completely satisfactory translation that accounts for every use of *Ioudaios* in John. In at least four instances, the term *Ioudaios* is used in a theologically neutral way (3:1; 7:15; 10:24; 11:36–37), and once it is even used of Jesus (4:9). In these instances, it would not make sense to render this phrase as "Jewish leader," though it would probably be a mistake to assume that the same negative understanding implied by other uses of *Ioudaios* is present. This means that there is no cookie-cutter approach to solving this issue. Second, as with most major problems we face in reading ancient texts in modern contexts, we must be content to search for a solution that solves the greatest number of problems while creating the fewest. Third, even if scholars were to reach a consensus on how to translate the phrase *hoi Ioudaioi* in John—which seems unlikely—we are still left with the interpretive difficulties raise by how *hoi Ioudaioi* are characterized in the gospel. We turn now to that problematic picture.

23. Ibid., 160, 165.

How Are *Ioudaioi* Portrayed?

It has already been stated that several instances of *Ioudaios* in John appear in contexts that are not inherently negative, but these are certainly the exception rather than the rule. Aside from the five brief scenes listed above, whenever the narrator discusses *hoi Ioudaioi*, the tone and context are decidedly negative. Here are some examples:

(1) In what is probably the most damning indictment in the narrative, Jesus tells "the Jews" that they are born of their father, the Devil:

> 42 Jesus said to them, "If God were your Father, you would love me, for I came from God and now I am here. I did not come on my own, but he sent me. 43 Why do you not understand what I say? It is because you cannot accept my word. 44 You are from your father the devil, and you choose to do your father's desires. He was a murderer from the beginning and does not stand in the truth, because there is no truth in him. When he lies, he speaks according to his own nature, for he is a liar and the father of lies. 45 But because I tell the truth, you do not believe me. 46 Which of you convicts me of sin? If I tell the truth, why do you not believe me? 47 Whoever is from God hears the words of God. The reason you do not hear them is that you are not from God." (John 8:42–47 NRSV)

(2) After Jesus heals the man born blind, "the Jews" challenge the young man. Consequently *they* appear to be blind and unable to see the truth:

> 24 So for the second time they called the man who had been blind, and they said to him, "Give glory to God! We know that this man is a sinner."

> 25 He answered, "I do not know whether he is a
> sinner. One thing I do know, that though I was
> blind, now I see." 26 They said to him, "What
> did he do to you? How did he open your eyes?"
> 27 He answered them, "I have told you already,
> and you would not listen. Why do you want to
> hear it again? Do you also want to become his
> disciples?" 28 Then they reviled him, saying,
> "You are his disciple, but we are disciples of Mo-
> ses. 29 We know that God has spoken to Moses,
> but as for this man, we do not know where he
> comes from." 30 The man answered, "Here is an
> astonishing thing! You do not know where he
> comes from, and yet he opened my eyes. 31 We
> know that God does not listen to sinners, but he
> does listen to one who worships him and obeys
> his will. 32 Never since the world began has it
> been heard that anyone opened the eyes of a
> person born blind. 33 If this man were not from
> God, he could do nothing." 34 They answered
> him, "You were born entirely in sins, and are
> you trying to teach us?" And they drove him
> out. (John 9:24–34 NRSV)

(3) "The Jews" are not only hostile toward Jesus but they do not remain true to their own theological beliefs and traditions:

> 31 The Jews took up stones again to stone him.
> 32 Jesus replied, "I have shown you many good
> works from the Father. For which of these are
> you going to stone me?" 33 The Jews answered,
> "It is not for a good work that we are going to
> stone you, but for blasphemy, because you,
> though only a human being, are making yourself
> God." 34 Jesus answered, "Is it not written in your
> law, 'I said, you are gods'? 35 If those to whom

> the word of God came were called 'gods'—and the scripture cannot be annulled—36 can you say that the one whom the Father has sanctified and sent into the world is blaspheming because I said, 'I am God's Son'? 37 If I am not doing the works of my Father, then do not believe me. 38 But if I do them, even though you do not believe me, believe the works, so that you may know and understand that the Father is in me and I am in the Father." 39 Then they tried to arrest him again, but he escaped from their hands (John 10:31–39 NRSV).

(4) After Jesus raises Lazarus from the dead, "the Jews" begin to plot Jesus' death:

> 45 Many of the Jews therefore, who had come with Mary and had seen what Jesus did, believed in him. 46 But some of them went to the Pharisees and told them what he had done. 47 So the chief priests and the Pharisees called a meeting of the council, and said, "What are we to do? This man is performing many signs. 48 If we let him go on like this, everyone will believe in him, and the Romans will come and destroy both our holy place and our nation." 49 But one of them, Caiaphas, who was high priest that year, said to them, "You know nothing at all! 50 You do not understand that it is better for you to have one man die for the people than to have the whole nation destroyed." 51 He did not say this on his own, but being high priest that year he prophesied that Jesus was about to die for the nation, 52 and not for the nation only, but to gather into one the dispersed children of God. 53 So from that day on they planned to put him to death. (John 11:45–53 NRSV)

(5) "The Jews" seek Jesus' crucifixion and ultimately succeed in bringing it about:

> 13 When Pilate heard these words, he brought Jesus outside and sat on the judge's bench at a place called The Stone Pavement, or in Hebrew Gabbatha. 14 Now it was the day of Preparation for the Passover; and it was about noon. He said to the Jews, "Here is your King!" 15 They cried out, "Away with him! Away with him! Crucify him!" Pilate asked them, "Shall I crucify your King?" The chief priests answered, "We have no king but the emperor." 16 Then he handed him over to them to be crucified. So they took Jesus; 17 and carrying the cross by himself, he went out to what is called The Place of the Skull, which in Hebrew is called Golgotha. 18 There they crucified him, and with him two others, one on either side, with Jesus between them. 19 Pilate also had an inscription written and put on the cross. It read, "Jesus of Nazareth, the King of the Jews." 20 Many of the Jews read this inscription, because the place where Jesus was crucified was near the city; and it was written in Hebrew, in Latin, and in Greek. 21 Then the chief priests of the Jews said to Pilate, "Do not write, 'The King of the Jews,' but, 'This man said, I am King of the Jews.'" 22 Pilate answered, "What I have written I have written." (John 19:13–22 NRSV)

The above examples represent only a limited selection of texts in which "the Jews" appear in an unflattering light, though these should suffice to demonstrate the pervasiveness of this perspective throughout the gospel. An awareness of this overall presentation raises the larger question of how to mitigate the tension of a Jewish writing that appears hostile toward "Jews." How can readers of John's Gospel approach this issue in a way that is sensitive to the historical, literary, and theological tensions that arise every time, "the Jews" are denigrated?

MITIGATING THE TENSION?

Often when I teach the Gospel of John, I find it necessary to point out that even though the gospel presents a sharp conflict between Jesus and the Jewish leaders, such a conflict is historically unlikely. The Jesus movement was likely not big enough during Jesus' lifetime for such a significant divide to have developed. In addition the strict dualism between Jesus on one end and "the Jews" on the other supports the gospel's dualistic emphasis and fails to account for the rich diversity that existed within Judaism in the first century. Instead, these elements of the narrative likely derive from the third stage of the gospel's development (see the discussion of these stages in chapter 3). On this point, George Smiga observes:

> It is historically dubious that Jesus' ministry evoked universal skepticism or rejection from the Jews of his time. The conflicts between Jesus and other Jews in the gospels have been colored by the issues of later Christian communities. The evangelists were inclined to identify their opponents with the opponents of Jesus. Thus the opponents of stage three were often inserted into a narrative that was describing stage one. As a result, Jesus' opponents in the written gospels do not reflect the diversity of Jewish groups that were active during his ministry.[24]

Practically, this means that when *hoi Ioudaioi* is used negatively, the phrase is functioning as a technical term for the

24. Smiga, *Gospel of John Set Free*, 5.

enemies of Jesus in the narrative rather than a historical or strictly ethnic designation. The phrase is more a reflection of the conflicts that arose during the time in which the gospel was written rather than something that took place during Jesus' historical context in the late 20s CE. Here is what we have tried to establish here and in the previous chapters: (1) the Johannine community is Jewish, but there has been some kind of conflict—likely an expulsion from the synagogue and by friends, all of whom are Jewish and locked in what John clearly regards as a closed religious system; (2) this conflict has been narrated through the two-level story that John tells (see chapter 3 for a fuller treatment of this subject); (3) in narrative terms, "the Jews" represent not any or all people of Jewish origin, but rather those who reject the revelation of God in and through Jesus. Rudolf Bultmann states it this way:

> The polemical situation [in the gospel] manifests a considerable change from that presupposed in the Synoptic Gospels. Admittedly in John, as in them, the Jews are in continual opposition to Jesus. But they no longer appear in the concrete distinctions of Palestinian relations, but always are described simply as "the Jews," in contrast to whom Jesus and his disciples appear as non-Jews (8.17; 10.34). In the Gospel of John the Jews represent the unbelieving world generally, and in the relations of the Jews to Jesus the relations of all unbelievers to the Christian Church and its message are mirrored.[25]

In other words, in John's dualistic conception of the *kosmos*, there are those who accept Jesus and those who reject him. There is no in-between, and those who reject Jesus—irrespective of their ethnicity—could likewise be

25. Bultmann, *Gospel of John*, 4.

designated as "Jews" in this economy. In historical terms, John's community had experienced rejection and exclusion by people who were, like themselves, ethnically Jewish. We are thus faced with an interpretive conundrum. By using the two-level approach discussed in the previous chapter, the historical author is reflecting on the experience of his community in turmoil but uses the (now unfortunate) title, "the Jews," to describe his opponents, even though he was also likely Jewish. All of this has created a serious problem in the history of interpretation. At its core, this issue is about John's narrative Christology, though the history of the community's experience has played a significant role in shaping how the story of rejection is narrated. Though this characterization of the Jewish leaders remains problematic, we are at least closer to understanding John's intent behind casting *hoi Ioudaioi* as those in opposition to Jesus. An informed and honest reading of the Gospel of John must take into account the troublesome tension that arises from paying attention to how "the Jews" are presented. Against that backdrop, I suggest that readers approach this issue in the text with at least four factors in mind:

(1) Recognize that in the vast number of instances, when the Gospel of John uses *hoi Ioudaioi*, it is referring specifically to the Jewish leaders and is functioning, literarily, as a technical term for Jesus' enemies.

(2) Recognize that *hoi Ioudaioi* does not refer to Jewish people as a representative group at any one time, and certainly not Jewish people of all time.

(3) Recognize that incalculable harm has been done to Jewish people in the name of Christianity, largely under the assumption that "the Jews" killed Jesus.

(4) Recognize the importance of keeping the concerns of ancient history and modern ethical concerns in a

necessary conversation when reading the Gospel of John.

Aware that the tension raised by John's complicated relationship to Judaism will never completely be resolved among readers, I close this chapter with a quote from Jewish New Testament scholar, Adele Reinhartz, with the hopes that it will provoke reflection in those who wish to become better and more perceptive readers of the Fourth Gospel:

> How, then, do we read our own sacred Scriptures? Do we read them in ways that serve only to accentuate the gulf between ourselves and others, or do we find ways to read them so as to honor rather than despair of the differences among us, and thereby transcend the legacy of hostility and violence that has bedeviled Jewish-Christian relations for centuries? Whether Jew, Christian, or neither, we are called upon to be thoughtful about our beloved and sacred stories, to engage with them seriously in a way that gives them honor but that also does not shirk from the difficult questions they may pose.[26]

REFLECTION:

1. How will an awareness of the historical and ethical problems addressed in this chapter impact your reading of the Gospel of John in the future?

2. How does the divide between Jesus and "the Jews" support the gospel's dualistic worldview?

26. Reinhartz, "Judaism in the Gospel of John," 393.

Chapter 5

AN ALIEN TONGUE

THE FOREIGN LANGUAGE OF THE JOHANNINE JESUS

THE 1984 SCI-FI FILM *Starman* tells the story of an alien who travels to Earth after intercepting the Voyager 2 space probe. Affixed to the probe is a gold record with a message of peace for all worlds and an invitation for the inhabitants of other galaxies to visit Earth. Arriving here in the form of a blue mass, the alien is shot down by the US government over rural Wisconsin. In order to survive his time on Earth, the alien uses a lock of hair to clone and take on the form of a recently deceased man named Scott Hayden (played by Jeff Bridges). After inhabiting Scott's body, "Starman"—as he comes to be called—enters the house formerly shared by Scott and his widow, Jenny (played by Karen Allen). Finding a naked man standing in her living room, Jenny mistakes him for an intruder and pulls her gun on him. When the intruder finally turns around, Jenny is astonished to see a man who looks exactly like her deceased husband. However, as the stranger begins to speak, Jenny realizes that this is not Scott, and she's not sure who (or even what) he is. She promptly faints in the corner—a moment of comic relief in an otherwise intense scene. Neither Starman's appearance nor his mannerisms give him away. But as soon as he begins to speak, it becomes clear that he is different, strange, alien. As the movie progresses Jenny comes to realize that Starman is from above—a stranger from the heavens—and that his mission is now to return safely to the place from which he came.

The story of Starman shares many similarities with John's presentation of Jesus: in like manner, Jesus has come from above (1:1–2) and taken on human flesh (1:14); his mission is to complete the tasks assigned to him by the Father and return to the place from which he came (e.g., 14:1–6); when Jesus speaks he introduces alien concepts and utters enigmatic sayings that are all-too-often misunderstood by his audiences, who presume he is from Galilee (e.g., 7:52), and find his words difficult to accept (e.g., 6:60–66; 10:31–33). This Jesus is not the gritty, earthy, Synoptic preacher of parables from rural Galilee. He is rather a stranger from heaven, who consistently speaks about the things above while mystifying his hearers.[1]

Very early in the history of Christianity, commentators recognized how drastically the Gospel of John differed from the other three canonical accounts. Around the year 200 CE, Clement of Alexandria wrote that John was "aware that the outward facts [about Jesus' life] had been set out in the [Synoptic] gospels," and that he was divinely motivated by the Holy Spirit to write "a *spiritual gospel*." One of the

1. In an influential and widely cited article from 1972, Wayne Meeks famously referred to the Johannine Jesus as the "man from heaven" (Meeks, "Man from Heaven in Johannine Sectarianism"). A few years later, Marinus de Jonge published a monograph in which he referred to John's Jesus as the "stranger from heaven" (*Jesus: Stranger from Heaven and Son of God*). Since the publication of these two works, it has become common among scholars to refer to the Johannine Jesus using these two phrases.

most strikingly different features of this "spiritual gospel" is the alien language used by Jesus. In this chapter we will examine closely the distinctiveness of Jesus' speech, with specific attention given to his "I am" pronouncements and the various types of ironic speech that appear in the gospel, including double entendre and misunderstood statements. We will also discuss other characteristic language and literary features used by the narrator of John's Gospel.

THE "I AM" STATEMENTS OF JESUS

As discussed in the previous chapter, John's view of Jesus is situated within a first-century Jewish framework. Against that backdrop, the Gospel of John provides an understanding of Jesus that moves beyond christological concerns expressed in the Synoptic tradition. One of the gospel's central themes is that Jesus is the unique representation of Israel's God to humanity (1:18). This theme is emphasized in numerous ways throughout the narrative, one of which is Jesus' consistent use of the phrase, "I am" (Greek: *egō eimi*) when speaking about himself. There is little doubt that this phrase is intended as a transparent allusion to the divine name, YHWH (also known as the "Tetragrammaton"; see table 5.1). Two types of "I am" pronouncements are found in the Gospel of John—absolute statements (sometimes called the un-predicated "I am" statements) and "I am" statements followed by a predicate.

Absolute "I Am" Statements

Much has been written about the absolute use of *egō eimi* in the Gospel of John. The Old Testament background of these pronouncements undeniably hearkens back to the revelation of God's name on Mount Horeb. In Exodus 3, Moses stands before a burning bush that is not consumed by its flames. Through this bush, the God of the Israelites speaks to Moses:

> I have observed the misery of my people who are in Egypt; I have heard their cry on account of their taskmasters. Indeed, I know their sufferings, and I have come down to deliver them from the Egyptians, and to bring them up out of that land to a good and broad land, a land flowing with milk and honey. . . . The cry of the Israelites has now come to me; I have also seen how the Egyptians oppress them. So come, I will send you to Pharaoh to bring my people, the Israelites, out of Egypt. (Exod 3:7–10 NRSV)

Somewhat skeptical, Moses asks, "If I come to the Israelites and say to them, 'The God of your ancestors has sent me to you,' and they ask me, 'What is his name?' what shall I say to them?" (3:13). God's response follows:

> "I am who I am." "Thus you shall say to the Israelites, 'I am has sent me to you.'" God also said to Moses, "Thus you shall say to the Israelites, 'The Lord, the God of your ancestors, the God of Abraham, the God of Isaac, and the God of Jacob, has sent me to you': This is my name forever, and this my title for all generations." (Exod 3:14–15 NRSV)

This passage, more than any other in the Old Testament, provides the foundation for our thinking about Jesus' use of "I am" in the Gospel of John. The phrase "I am who I am" (Hebrew: *ehyeh ehyeh*; Exod 3:14) can also be translated, "I am that I am," or possibly, "I will be what I will be." The divine name, which God reveals to Moses is YHWH (sometimes spelled Yahweh), a form of the Hebrew verb *hayah*, "to be." Within traditional Jewish thinking, YHWH is quite simply "the God who is."

As discussed in chapter 2, the Greek version of the Old Testament, also known as the Septuagint, was the Bible used by most of the authors of the New Testament (for more information, refer back to table 2.1). In Greek, the

TABLE 5.1

YHWH: The Name of Israel's God

The name Yahweh is most often spelled in four uppercase letters as a reflection of the practice in the original Hebrew text. Some refer to this appearance of the name as the "Tetragrammaton"—Greek for "four letters." The Hebrew language did not originally have vowels; the script was written in a consonant-only text in letters known today as radicals. Since vocal inflection was understood by those who spoke the language, there was no need to write the vowels. However, there eventually came a time when Hebrew no longer existed as a spoken language. Between the 5th and 7th centuries CE, a group known as the Masoretes invented vowel markings for the Hebrew language so that readers would better understand the Scriptures. Today this version of the Hebrew Bible is known as the Masoretic text.

Even after the vowel markings were added to the Hebrew text, the name Yahweh was either retained as four consonants (יהוה), or more often appeared with the vowel markings belonging to the Hebrew term *adonai* (= lord, master). This was done to prevent people from casually reading or speaking the name of God aloud. Those "in the know" understood that this word was to be pronounced *adonai* to avoid any sacrilege; those who were ignorant of this convention accidentally created a corruption of the divine name by pronouncing it *Jehovah*. Another way of avoiding the casual use of God's name was simply to refer to God using the Hebrew term *ha shēm* ("the name"). All of this was done to protect the sanctity of God's name in both religious and social discourse.

phrase *egō eimi* is used to translate the Hebrew verb *hayah* in Exod 3:14. The Gospel of John is thus reaching back into the Exodus story to make a connection between the identity of Jesus and the name of God. As transparent as this allusion is, it is only one of several instances in which the phrase *egō eimi* is used as a substitute for the divine name employed in the Hebrew tradition.

Confessing the name of God was central to the life and worship of pious Jews in the first century, though they often went out of their way to avoid speaking the divine name, both in public and in private (for more, see table 5.1 above). Over time, reverence for the name of God within Judaism led to its abandonment in social and religious discourse. As a result, religious Jews began to use the phrase "I am he" (Hebrew: *ani hu* / *anoki hu*) as a substitute. This phrase can be found in a number of passages in the Old Testament, the most important of which appear in Isaiah:

1. Isa 43:10: "You are my witnesses," says the Lord, "and my servant whom I have chosen, in order that you might know and believe that *I am* (he) [Hebrew: *ani hu*; Greek: *egō eimi*]. No god was formed before me and there shall be none after me."
2. Isa 43:25: "I am, *I am* (he) [Hebrew: *anoki anoki hu*; Greek *egō eimi egō eimi*] who blots out transgressions for my own sake and will remember your sins no more."
3. Isa 48:12: "Hear me O Jacob, and Israel whom I have called: *I am* (he) [Hebrew: *ani hu* ; Greek: *egō eimi*]. I am the first and I am the last."
4. Isa 52:6: "Therefore, my people will know my name, thus, on that day, that *I am* (he) [Hebrew: *ani hu*; Greek: *egō eimi*] is speaking. Behold, here I am."

In each of these instances, the Hebrew phrase "I am he" is translated with an absolute *egō eimi* in the Septuagint. Here we have further evidence that the absolute use of *egō eimi* was a specific designation for the divine name, YHWH. In light of this cumulative evidence, it seems clear that John's absolute use of *egō eimi* is intended as an explicit reference to the divine name. I argued above that according to the Prologue, the *Logos* also possesses the name of God (see n17 in ch. 2). Jesus' use of absolute "I am" statements carries this idea from the first few lines of John's Gospel throughout the remainder of the story.

Now that we have discussed its significance, it remains to show how this construction functions in specific texts. Altogether, the absolute use of *egō eimi* appears nine times in six different passages:

1. Jesus in conversation with the Samaritan woman (4:25–26):

> 25 The woman said to him, "I know that Messiah is coming" (who is called Christ). "When he comes, he will proclaim all things to us." 26 Jesus said to her, "I am [*egō eimi*], the one who is speaking to you."

2. Jesus walks on the water before his disciples (6:19–21):

> 19 When they had rowed about three or four miles, they saw Jesus walking on the sea and coming near the boat, and they were terrified. 20 But he said to them, "I am [*egō eimi*] do not be afraid."

3. Jesus speaking to the Jewish leaders and the crowds (8:24–30):

> 24 I told you that you would die in your sins, for you will die in your sins unless you believe that I am [*egō eimi*]." 25 They said to him, "Who are you?" Jesus said to them, "Why do I speak to you at all? 26 I have much to say about you

> and much to condemn; but the one who sent me is true, and I declare to the world what I have heard from him." 27 They did not understand that he was speaking to them about the Father. 28 So Jesus said, "When you have lifted up the Son of Man, then you will realize that I am [*egō eimi*], and that I do nothing on my own, but I speak these things as the Father instructed me.

4. Jesus and the Jewish leaders discuss Abraham (8:54–59):

> 54 Jesus answered, "If I glorify myself, my glory is nothing. It is my Father who glorifies me, he of whom you say, 'He is our God,' 55 though you do not know him. But I know him; if I would say that I do not know him, I would be a liar like you. But I do know him and I keep his word. 56 Your ancestor Abraham rejoiced that he would see my day; he saw it and was glad." 57 Then the Jews said to him, "You are not yet fifty years old, and have you seen Abraham?" 58 Jesus said to them, "Amen amen, I say to you, before Abraham was, I am [*egō eimi*]." 59 So they picked up stones to throw at him, but Jesus hid himself and went out of the temple.

5. Jesus washes the feet of his disciples (13:16–20):

> 16 Amen amen, I say to you, servants are not greater than their master, nor are messengers greater than the one who sent them. 17 If you know these things, you are blessed if you do them. 18 I am not speaking of all of you; I know whom I have chosen. But it is to fulfill the scripture, "The one who ate my bread has lifted his heel against me." 19 I tell you this now, before it occurs, so that when it does occur, you may believe that I am [*egō eimi*]. 20 Amen amen, I say to you, whoever receives one whom I send

> receives me; and whoever receives me receives him who sent me.

6. Jesus is arrested in the garden (18:3–9):

> 3 So Judas brought a detachment of soldiers together with police from the chief priests and the Pharisees, and they came there with lanterns and torches and weapons. 4 Then Jesus, knowing all that was to happen to him, came forward and asked them, "For whom are you looking?" 5 They answered, "Jesus of Nazareth." Jesus replied, "I am [*egō eimi*]." Judas, who betrayed him, was standing with them. 6 When Jesus said to them, "I am [*egō eimi*]," they stepped back and fell to the ground. 7 Again he asked them, "Whom are you looking for?" And they said, "Jesus of Nazareth." 8 Jesus answered, "I told you that I am [*egō eimi*]. So if you are looking for me, let these men go." 9 This was to fulfill the word that he had spoken, "I did not lose a single one of those whom you gave me."

In each of the above passages, Jesus uses *egō eimi* to emphasize something about his identity and mission. Some occurrences of the phrase are more explicitly related to Jesus' identity than others (e.g., 8:58), though each is intended to connect with the reader and highlight something that has already been revealed. The implied reader of John's Gospel has read the Prologue and knows of Jesus' connection to the God of Israel. In these pronouncements the reader now witnesses the voice of Jesus confirming what only the voice of the narrator had previously announced.

This unique christological emphasis differs from the portraits of Jesus in the Synoptic Gospels in two important respects. First, in the Synoptic accounts, Jesus appears to become progressively aware of his mission and identity, whereas here, he is fully aware of his identity from the start and knows how this impacts his relationship to the Father. Second, in Matthew, Mark, and Luke, Jesus is called Messiah, Son of Man, and Son of God, but at no point is he explicitly identified as divine. While some argue that Jesus should be understood as possessing divine status in the Synoptic Gospels, only in John is this clearly spelled out for the reader.

Predicated "I Am" Statements

A second type of "I am" sayings appears on the lips of Jesus, and each of these introduces a specific title. These sayings appear with a predicate—that portion of the sentence which excludes the subject. This formulation has led scholars to label these as "predicated" or "predicative" *egō eimi* statements. Since many readers of this book will have long forgotten their elementary school grammar, a brief refresher will prove helpful.

In the basic sentence, "the boy has the ball," the subject is "the boy" while the remainder of the sentence (in this case, the verb and direct object) constitutes the predicate. The subject and the predicate are the two essential building blocks of any sentence. In each of the predicated "I am" statements, Jesus uses the formula, "I am X" (where "am X" = the predicate). Each predicate introduces a title that is reminiscent of an important image from Israel's story (see table 5.2 below for a full list of these sayings). In his detailed study of "I am" formulations in John, David Mark Ball notes that each predicated saying appeals to something of religious significance in the Old Testament:

> Jesus claims to be the Bread of which the Old Testament spoke, the Light of which Isaiah spoke, the Shepherd of whom Jeremiah and Ezekiel spoke, and the Vine of which many Old

> Testament passages spoke. In addition there may be allusions to the Isaianic concept of the "way of the LORD" in Jesus' claim to be the Way, the Truth and Life. Jesus also takes the Jewish concept of resurrection of which Martha speaks and transforms it to refer to the present in his own person (11.25). In these sayings it is not the words "I am" which are found in the Old Testament, but the images which accompany them. The words *egō eimi* thus act as a formula which applies Old Testament and Jewish concepts to the person of Jesus who embodies and fulfils them.[2]

In other words, in their predicated form, the "I am" sayings are christological in nature, but they are not meant to claim for Jesus a divine status like the absolute sayings. Rather a connection to some important image or theme from Israel's Scriptures is in view. Further, each image—bread, vine, shepherd, etc.—represents something positive that Jesus does for those who believe. Thus, the predicated "I am" sayings are more than christological, they speak directly to Jesus' relationship with his followers; they "emphasize the relationship between Jesus and believers . . . and also suggest that John connected Christology closely with early Christian experience."[3]

2. Ball, *"I Am" in John's Gospel*, 259. About this second type of pronouncement, Keener notes the predicative "I am" statements are "more christological than ecclesiological. Granted, the latter was by this period a serious issue; but for John, ecclesiology is determined entirely by Christology, because the community is defined solely by allegiance to Christ, who is the only way to the Father (14:6)." Keener, *Gospel of John*, 1:318.

3. Keener, *Gospel of John*, 1:318, 320.

IRONY

The Oxford English Dictionary defines irony as the "expression of one's meaning by using language that normally signifies the opposite, typically for humorous or emphatic effect." Irony is a technique often employed in literature (as well as in television and film) that allows for a shared experience of meaning between a storyteller and the audience, of which the other characters in a story are usually not aware. In the Gospel of John, Jesus and the narrator both engage in this practice, generating verbal and situational ironies. Most often in John, these ironies arise through the use of double entendre and misunderstood statements. We will examine how these two conventions work in concert with one another.

Double entendre results when ambiguous language is used to create an expression that can have more than one interpretation. In modern contexts, double entendre often has one innocuous meaning and a secondary meaning that is suggestive of something deeper. We can illustrate the type of double entendre we see in John with an example from the 1991 film *Silence of the Lambs*. In his Academy Award-winning role, Anthony Hopkins plays Hannibal Lecter, a sociopath psychiatrist who kills and eats his patients—a practice which gives rise to his notorious moniker, "Hannibal the Cannibal." Toward the end of the film, Hannibal escapes police custody and finds himself on the run. While still a fugitive, Hannibal places a telephone call to Clarice, the film's main character (played by Jodie Foster). As their conversation draws to a close, Hannibal spots Dr. Frederick Chilton, the man who had been in charge of him during his imprisonment. He quickly closes the conversation with these words: "I do wish we could chat longer, but I'm having an old friend for dinner." Any viewer who has been paying attention is struck with an immediate sense of fear, but also likely finds Hannibal's turn of a phrase a little humorous. Typically the expression Hannibal uses here means something like, "I'm going to have an old friend over to my house so that we can dine together." However in this case, it means that Hannibal (the Cannibal!) will literally be having Dr. Chilton for his meal. This example is similar to the type of double entendre we see in John.

TABLE 5.2

The Predicated *egō eimi* Statements in the Gospel of John

"I am the bread of life" (6:35, 48)
"I am the bread/ living bread which came down from heaven" (6:41, 51)
"I am the light of the world" (8:12)
"I am the gate / I am the gate for the sheep" (10:7, 9)
"I am the good shepherd" (10:11, 14)
"I am the resurrection and the life" (11:25)
"I am the way, the truth, and the life" (14:6)
"I am the vine/ true vine" (15:1, 5)

One of the difficulties in appreciating the way John makes use of this literary technique is that in order to understand some of these wordplays, one must know something about the Greek language. Since most modern readers of the Bible know very little about the original language of the NT, these sophisticated double meanings are often missed. Even more problematic is that most of our English translations are forced to settle for one specific rendering of a particular word, which means that the intentional ambiguity can be lost. Nowhere is the phenomenon of double entendre, along with the problem of translation, more apparent than in John 3.

In one of the most well-known passages of the NT, a religious leader named Nicodemus approaches Jesus by night. Their interaction unfolds as follows:

> 1 Now there was a Pharisee named Nicodemus,
> a leader of the Jews. 2 He came to him by night
> and said to him, "Rabbi, we know that you are a teacher who has come from God; for no one can do these signs that you do apart from the presence of God." 3 Jesus answered him, "Very truly,
> I tell you, no one can see the kingdom of God without being born *anōthen*." 4 Nicodemus said
> to him, "How can anyone be born after having grown old? Can one enter a second time into the mother's womb and be born?" (NRSV)

Many modern readers of the New Testament will immediately recognize this passage and will intuitively know that Jesus has just spoken to Nicodemus about being "born again." However, in the text above I have chosen to retain the Greek word (*anōthen*) as a way of highlighting the ambiguity at work here. The primary meaning of *anōthen* is "from above," and this appears to be in keeping with how Jesus is using the word. He is speaking on a higher plane about things of a spiritual nature. However, a misplaced literalism leads Nicodemus to understand *anōthen* as "again" or "anew"—a secondary and less common use of the term. Jesus is trying to help Nicodemus understand what it means to be born from above but Nicodemus can only conceive of birth physically, so he raises a question that borders on the ludicrous: "How can anyone be born after having grown old? Can one enter a second time into the mother's womb and be born?" (v. 4). The reader understands what Nicodemus does not. Jesus has come from above (cf. 1:1–2) and therefore speaks as one from above. Nicodemus's focus on the literal creates this misunderstanding and again places the reader in a position of privilege.

Table 5.3

Nicodemus Misunderstands Jesus

Jesus speaks on a higher, spiritual plane

anōthen = "born from above" = spiritual rebirth

Nicodemus interprets on a lower, literal plane

anōthen = "born again" = literal rebirth

From the Prologue, the reader knows what characters in the narrative have yet to learn. Double entendre is used throughout the gospel, often in contexts of character formation where misunderstanding is expressed. When a given character displays this type of misunderstanding, the implied reader perceives the error in question and either gains a new insight or has a previous insight confirmed.

Another example of this type of double entendre occurs in Jesus' conversation with the woman of Samaria (4:7–42). Before we look at their interaction it will prove helpful to examine the intentional contrasts between Jesus' conversations with Nicodemus (John 3) and the Samaritan woman (John 4). The reader is supposed to pick up on some of the subtle and not-so-subtle differences between these two situations. First, the most obvious difference between these two figures is in their respective genders. Second, Nicodemus is a man of high social status. He is identified as a Pharisee and member of the Jewish ruling council. The woman of Samaria, we soon find out, has had five husbands and is now cohabiting with a man that is not her husband; it's safe to say that this reality has caused her to be relegated to the margins of society. Third, Nicodemus is a Jew while the woman is a Samaritan. Fourth, the reader knows Nicodemus's name while the woman remains nameless. Fifth and finally, Nicodemus approaches Jesus by night while the conversation between Jesus and the Samaritan woman takes place at midday. These temporal indicators in the narrative are especially significant for shaping our understanding of both interactions. As stated above, Nicodemus comes to Jesus under the cover of night, which is likely symbolic of two things: (1) his unwillingness to make his interest in Jesus known in the daylight, and (2) his status as one shrouded in darkness and misunderstanding (cf. 1:5). By contrast, the woman of Samaria appears at the well in the middle of the day, which speaks to her marginalized status. In general, women would gather together in the morning or early evening to draw water, thus providing both camaraderie and safety in numbers. However, this woman is alone at the well during the hottest part of the day. We are to understand her as a marginalized figure who, for reasons yet to be divulged, is not welcome in the daily corporate gatherings at the well. While these details are not explicitly spelled out, this narrative gap invites the reader to fill in information as more insights are provided into the woman's situation. The conversation begins as follows:

> 7 A Samaritan woman came to draw water, and
> Jesus said to her, "Give me a drink." 8 (His dis-
> ciples had gone to the city to buy food.) 9 The
> Samaritan woman said to him, "How is it that
> you, a Jew, ask a drink of me, a woman of Samaria?" (Jews do not share things in common
> with Samaritans.) 10 Jesus answered her, "If you
> knew the gift of God, and who it is that is saying to you, 'Give me a drink,' you would have
> asked him, and he would have given you living
> water." 11 The woman said to him, "Sir, you have
> no bucket, and the well is deep. Where do you
> get that living water? 12 Are you greater than our
> ancestor Jacob, who gave us the well, and with

> his sons and his flocks drank from it?" 13 Jesus said to her, "Everyone who drinks of this water will be thirsty again, 14 but those who drink of the water that I will give them will never be thirsty. The water that I will give will become in them a spring of water gushing up to eternal life." 15 The woman said to him, "Sir, give me this water, so that I may never be thirsty or have to keep coming here to draw water." (NRSV)

The conversation between Jesus and the woman initially revolves around water, having been sparked by Jesus' request for something to drink (v. 7). Incredulous at his request, the woman replies: "How is it that you, a Jew, ask a drink of me, a woman of Samaria?" (v. 9). These words are followed by a reminder from the narrator that the Jews and Samaritans are generally at odds with one another. Jesus responds by saying, "If you knew the gift of God, and who it is that is saying to you, 'Give me a drink,' you would have asked him, and he would have given you *living water* [Greek: *hydōr zōn*]" (v. 10). Here again, Jesus is speaking on a higher, otherworldly plane about water which imparts life. He does not have in mind literal water, even though the conversation is taking place at a well in a context in which literal water has been discussed. However, the woman is clearly interested in literal water, which is why she has come to the well in the first place. Complicating matters further is that the phrase "living water" was used in Greek as a euphemism for "running water," (as opposed to stale water from a cistern), and this is how the Samaritan woman understands Jesus' words. Her next question ("Sir, you have no bucket, and the well is deep. Where do you get that *living water*?" v. 11) and her request ("Sir, give me this water, so that I may never be thirsty or have to keep coming here to draw water," v. 15) both betray her misplaced literalism. She is hoping for real water so that she can avoid coming to the well alone at midday—a continual reminder of her shame and marginal status. However, the water Jesus promises is figurative. As with Nicodemus, Jesus is offering the Samaritan woman something greater.

Table 5.4

The Samaritan Woman Misunderstands Jesus

Jesus speaks on a higher, spiritual plane

→

hydōr zōn = a metaphorical phrase indicating "water which imparts life"

The Samartian interprets on a lower, literal plane

→

hydōr zōn = "running water" = literal water

Throughout the Gospel of John, double entendre is employed in a number of ways. First, it is used to confound characters and give expression to veiled mysteries, while reinforcing for the reader truths about Jesus that have been revealed in the Prologue. Second, it is also used to add theological depth to a description of Jesus and his mission (see the discussion of 1:5 in table 5.5, below). This device is used both by the narrator and the Johannine Jesus in a way that serves the overall theological rhetoric of the gospel.

Table 5.5

Other Examples of Irony in the Gospel of John

1:5: "The light shines in the darkness and the darkness has not understood/overcome it."

The Greek term used here is *katalambanō*, which can be used of comprehending as well as overcoming. It is functioning ironically here, because both nuances prove to be true as the narrative progresses; those who are shrouded in darkness fail to understand Jesus and while the forces of darkness attempt to overcome Jesus, they ultimately fail.

7:33–36: Jesus said, "I am with you for only a short time, and then I am going to the one who sent me. You will look for me, but you will not find me; and where I am, you cannot come." The Jews said to one another, "Where does this man intend to go that we cannot find him? Will he go where our people live scattered among the Greeks, and teach the Greeks? What did he mean when he said, 'You will look for me, but you will not find me,' and "Where I am, you cannot come'?"

The reader knows that Jesus has come from above and that, as part of his mission, he must return to the Father. Against the backdrop of this knowledge, the reader is supposed to find the question of the Jewish leaders ironic, and a little humorous.

11:49–50: "Then one of them, named Caiaphas, who was high priest that year, spoke up, 'You know nothing at all! You do not realize that it is better for you that one man die for the people than that the whole nation perish.'"

Caiaphas is speaking out of opposition to Jesus, about what is good for the nation. His point is that it is better for the Romans to punish Jesus for his teachings, than for all of Israel to suffer at the hands of the Romans. However, this statement is ironic because the reader knows that part of Jesus' mission as one man is to die on behalf of the people.

There are numerous other instances of irony in John. For further reading on this topic, see Paul D. Duke, *Irony in the Fourth Gospel*.

Hand-in-hand with double entendre is the gospel's emphasis on misunderstanding. Not only is misunderstanding a key theme throughout the gospel, but Johannine irony—especially as it is expressed through double entendre—cannot work apart from characters who interact with and misunderstand Jesus. Here are a few examples:

1. Jesus' opponents mistakenly believe he is referring to the Jerusalem temple when he is speaking metaphorically about his own body (2:13–21):

> 13 The Passover of the Jews was near, and Jesus went up to Jerusalem. 14 In the temple he found people selling cattle, sheep, and doves, and the money changers seated at their tables. 15 Making a whip of cords, he drove all of them out of the temple, both the sheep and the cattle. He also poured out the coins of the money changers and overturned their tables. 16 He told those who were selling the doves, "Take these things out of here! Stop making my Father's house a marketplace!" 17 His disciples remembered that it was written, "Zeal for your house will consume me." 18 The Jews then said to him, "What sign can you show us for doing this?" 19 Jesus answered them, "Destroy this temple, and in three days I will raise it up." 20 The Jews then said, "This temple has been under construction for forty-six years, and will you raise it up in three days?" 21 But he was speaking of the temple of his body. (NRSV)

As the narrator points out in v. 21, Jesus uses the phrase "this temple" in reference to his physical body, and his opponents react with derision because they mistakenly believe that he is talking about the Jewish temple in Jerusalem. As with other instances of double entendre, a misplaced literalism—in this case, a focus on the Jerusalem temple—leads to misunderstanding. Not all examples of character misunderstanding occur in the same context in which double entendre is used, though here (as with the two examples cited above) the two are found working together.

2. "Many disciples" leave after Jesus announces that followers must "eat my flesh" and "drink my blood" (6:52–59, 66):

> 52 The Jews then disputed among themselves, saying, "How can this man give us his flesh to eat?" 53 So Jesus said to them, "Very truly, I tell you, unless you eat the flesh of the Son of Man and drink his blood, you have no life in you. 54 Those who eat my flesh and drink my blood have eternal life, and I will raise them up on the last day; 55 for my flesh is true food and my blood is true drink. 56 Those who eat my flesh and drink my blood abide in me, and I in them. 57 Just as the living Father sent me, and I live because of the Father, so whoever eats me will live because of me. 58 This is the bread that came down from heaven, not like that which your ancestors ate, and they died. But the one who eats this bread will live forever." 59 He said these things while he was teaching in the synagogue at Capernaum. . . . 66 Because of this many of his disciples turned back and no longer went about with him. (NRSV)

Unlike the Synoptic Gospels, the Gospel of John does not have an explicit passage in which Jesus institutes the tradition that later became known as the "Eucharist" or "Lord's Supper." However, it is quite widely recognized that standing behind Jesus' teaching in John 6 is a tradition related to the Eucharist. Returning to our discussion from chapter 3, we must acknowledge that some elements of the gospel were meant specifically for the original readers from the

Johannine community; material from John 6 likely represents one of those places. In proclaiming that followers must eat his flesh and drink his blood, Jesus is not referring to cannibalism. Rather, Jesus has in mind a spiritually-sustaining Eucharistic meal in which the earliest Johannine Christians participated. The disciples who depart are, like the characters in previous examples, guilty of a misplaced literalism, but the earliest readers of the Fourth Gospel knew that behind this teaching was one of their most cherished acts of worship.

3. The Disciples misunderstand Jesus' statement that Lazarus has "fallen asleep" (11:7–14):

> 7 Then after this he said to the disciples, "Let us
> go to Judea again." 8 The disciples said to him,
> "Rabbi, the Jews were just now trying to stone
> you, and are you going there again?" 9 Jesus an-
> swered, "Are there not twelve hours of daylight?
> Those who walk during the day do not stumble,
> because they see the light of this world. 10 But
> those who walk at night stumble, because the
> light is not in them." 11 After he had said this,
> he went on to tell them, "Our friend Lazarus has
> fallen asleep; but I am going there to wake him
> up." 12 His disciples replied, "Lord, if he sleeps,
> he will get better." 13 Jesus had been speaking
> of his death, but his disciples thought he meant
> natural sleep. 14 Then Jesus told them plainly,
> "Lazarus is dead." (NRSV)

Jesus and the disciples have already been to Judea and experienced the very real threat of death at the hands of those who oppose them. In this passage Jesus announces his intent to return to Judea, a location the Twelve now appropriately associate with death (see Thomas's comment in 11:16). However, Jesus' mission to Judea will ultimately be characterized by life as he raises Lazarus from the dead (see 11:38–44). This scene is dripping with irony as the reader anticipates Jesus' life-giving actions at the tomb of Lazarus, while the disciples are hung up on dying in Judea. However, the greater irony here is that even though the disciples associate their impending trip to Judea with death, they fail to understand a commonly used and quite transparent metaphor for death: sleep. Their commitment to the literal meaning of "falling sleep" causes them to miss Jesus' point about Lazarus's death, and so they reply that Lazarus will eventually wake up (v. 12). In the face of their incomprehension, Jesus plainly tells them in v. 14 that Lazarus has died.

4. The disciples fail to understand the significance of Judas leaving the meal (13:18–28):

> 18 "I am not speaking of all of you; I know
> whom I have chosen. But it is to fulfill the scripture, 'The one who ate my bread has lifted his
> heel against me.' 19 I tell you this now, before
> it occurs, so that when it does occur, you may
> believe that I am he. 20 Very truly, I tell you,
> whoever receives one whom I send receives me;
> and whoever receives me receives him who sent
> me." 21 After saying this Jesus was troubled in
> spirit, and declared, "Very truly, I tell you, one
> of you will betray me." 22 The disciples looked at
> one another, uncertain of whom he was speaking. 23 One of his disciples—the one whom Jesus loved—was reclining next to him; 24 Simon
> Peter therefore motioned to him to ask Jesus of
> whom he was speaking. 25 So while reclining
> next to Jesus, he asked him, "Lord, who is it?" 26
> Jesus answered, "It is the one to whom I give this
> piece of bread when I have dipped it in the dish."
> So when he had dipped the piece of bread, he

> gave it to Judas son of Simon Iscariot. [27] After he received the piece of bread, Satan entered into him. Jesus said to him, "Do quickly what you are going to do." [28] Now no one at the table knew why he said this to him. (NRSV)

The audience already knows that Judas is the one who will betray Jesus. This has been stated explicitly in 6:71. The disciples are unaware of this inside information, so they are troubled by Jesus' prediction of betrayal. Jesus openly states that the betrayer is the one to whom he will give a piece of bread (v. 26), after which he immediately hands the morsel to Judas (v. 27). Jesus then utters the cryptic command, "Do quickly what you are going to do." Not surprisingly, this event fails to set off any alarms among the notoriously dense disciples who, we are told, do not understand why Jesus spoke to Judas in this way.

Other instances of misunderstanding appear throughout the narrative, though the examples provided above should suffice to demonstrate John's use of this literary technique. We will discuss character misunderstanding in greater detail in the next chapter. For now, the focus is on how Jesus' alien speech is used as a vehicle to create misunderstanding while communicating directly with the reader who has been elevated by means of exposure to the information revealed in the Prologue.

DOUBLE AMEN SAYINGS

Another feature of Johannine discourse is Jesus' consistent use of amen to introduce his sayings. The term amen ("verily," "truly") was brought over into Greek from Hebrew, where it was most commonly used by an outside party to affirm the truthfulness of a given statement. Jesus' use of amen is unique in two respects: (1) Jesus, rather than an outside party is applying amen to his own sayings; and (2) Jesus is *introducing* his sayings with amen rather *appending it to the end*. The reader should understand that this phrase is used by Jesus to affirm the truthfulness of his words. The practice of beginning a pronouncement with amen is attested in the Synoptic Gospels,[4] though a major difference

Table 5.6

Some Examples of the Double Amen in John

1:51: "Amen, amen I say to you, you will see heaven opened and the angels of God ascending and descending upon the Son of Man."

3:5: "Amen, amen I say to you, no one can enter the kingdom of God unless they are born of water and the Spirit."

5:19: "Amen, amen I say to you, the Son can do nothing by himself; he can do only what he sees his Father doing, because whatever the Father does the Son also does."

6:32: "Amen, amen I say to you, it is not Moses who has given you the bread from heaven, but it is my Father who gives you the true bread from heaven."

8:34: "Amen, amen I say to you, everyone who sins is a slave to sin."

12:24: "Amen, amen I say to you, unless a grain of wheat falls to the ground and dies, it remains only a single seed. But if it dies, it produces many seeds."

16:23: "Amen, amen I say to you, my Father will give you whatever you ask in my name."

See also 3:3, 11; 5:24, 25; 6:26, 47, 53; 8:51, 58; 10:1, 7; 13:16, 20, 21, 38; 14:12; 16:20; 21:18.

4. The single amen is used to introduce a pronouncement thirty-one times in Matthew, thirteen times in Mark, and six times in Luke.

is that in John Jesus uses a double amen to introduce his sayings. The twenty-five instances of this double amen formula are often rendered, "truly truly," "very truly," or "most assuredly," in modern English translations; the King James Version uses "verily verily." I have chosen to keep "amen amen" in the examples in Table 5.6 in order to preserve the strangeness of phrase.

LITERARY ASIDES

When reading the Gospel of John, you will occasionally encounter places in the story where the narrator turns directly to the audience to explain the meaning or significance of a given detail. In the theater, when a character in the drama interrupts the time and space of the story world to speak directly to the audience, this is known as an "aside." We see a similar phenomenon in the Gospel of John, which one scholar has described as "explanatory material which is not directly involved in the progress of the narrative."[5] Everyone agrees that these literary asides occur, but there is fairly significant disagreement over what constitutes such an interruption and how many actually appear in John. Most English translations set these comments in parentheses, but this is ultimately an interpretive decision. Since the original manuscripts had nothing similar to parentheses, translators must base such decisions on their own overall reading of the narrative.

Depending upon which English translation you use, you will find either a few or many places in the gospel where parenthetical notations are used. Since different scholars set forth different criteria for what constitutes one of these asides, it is impossible to provide here an exhaustive list of their appearances in John (for various proposals, see the

5. Tenney, "Footnotes of John's Gospel," 350.

articles listed in table 5.7, below). However, the use of these literary asides provides unique insights into two elements of the reading process already discussed—one literary and the other historical.

Table 5.7

Literary Asides in John*

*indicated here by parentheses

1:41–42: He first found his brother Simon and said to him, "We have found the Messiah" (*which is translated Anointed*). He brought Simon to Jesus, who looked at him and said, "You are Simon son of John. You are to be called Cephas" (*which is translated Peter*).

2:9: When the steward tasted the water that had become wine, and did not know where it came from (*though the servants who had drawn the water knew*), the steward called the bridegroom.

4:9: The Samaritan woman said to him, "How is it that you, a Jew, ask a drink of me, a woman of Samaria?" (*Jews do not share things in common with Samaritans.*)

4:25: The woman said to him, "I know that Messiah is coming" (*who is called Christ*).

For other possible examples, see the competing proposals offered by O'Rourke, "Asides in the Gospel of John," and Thatcher, "A New Look at Asides in the Fourth Gospel."

First, readers of the gospel have been exposed to the comprehensive information provided in the Prologue. We have already argued that this information serves as an audience-elevating device that puts the reader in the position of having greater knowledge than most characters in the story. This does not mean, however, that the reader is omniscient, as is clear from the narrator's need to inform the reader of the significance of various details. These asides show one way in which the highly-informed audience continues to learn throughout the story. Second, the audience for whom this gospel was originally intended actually existed in history (see Starting Point 1 in chapter 1). The author(s) of the Fourth Gospel obviously felt the need to explain specific details to the intended audience, which can help provide clues as to the makeup of that original audience.

REFLECTION:

1. How does an appreciation of the gospel's unique language help you understand the Christology of John's Gospel? What does this type of language communicate about Jesus' identity and mission?

2. After reading this chapter, go back and read the words of Jesus in one or more of the Synoptic Gospels. How does the language differ from account to account? What do these differences tell you about the unique theological message and emphases of the Fourth Gospel?

Chapter 6

JOHN'S CHARACTERS AND THE RHETORIC OF MISUNDERSTANDING

I WAS BORN INTO a family of readers and along with my wife I have helped reproduce a family of readers. As a child, I remember my house being covered on all sides by shelves lined, top to bottom, with books. The Harvard Classics, instructional manuals, historical fiction, Shakespearean comedies—all of these called to me from the walls of my childhood home. To this day, I can still close my eyes and visualize the particular artwork on dozens of dust jackets that would catch my eye as I darted from room to room. My mother was an avid reader and so not surprisingly, I married an avid reader. My wife—a book lover and elementary reading teacher—is generally a happy-go-lucky individual. However, there is one certain way to usher her into an almost instantaneous depression: give her a good book series and allow her to make a genuine connection with its characters. That sounds harmless enough, I admit, but as soon as she has finished reading the series she will begin moping around the house like a woman in mourning. Over the next few days we will find her staring into space, looking lost.

When we ask her what's wrong she will say something like, "I've lost my friends," or, "I feel like my friends have left me." (Did I mention that she *really* likes to read?)

Few elements of a story can capture our imagination and help us see the world around us in new and different ways like characters can. Through characters we are able to make a connection to an experience we have had or hope to have. When we read we not only see ourselves but we see others we have known in the characters we encounter. Anyone who has done much reading knows that character development—especially as it relates to a character's inner-life—is an important element in much contemporary writing. The construction of personal identity is important to modern individuals and therefore plays an important role in the modern novel. When we encounter characters in contemporary literature, we are often treated to the inner psychological life of figures who move toward (and in some cases away from) moments of redemption. As familiar as all of this is to readers of modern literature, this is not how characters typically functioned in ancient literature. Therefore, when approaching characters of the Bible we must be careful to situate them within the thought worlds that gave rise to them.

In ancient literature, action was generally considered the most important element in any dramatic presentation. The practical outworking of this model is that the figure performing the action was nearly always secondary to the action being performed.[1] When we subjugate the interests of characters to the action of a story, those characters can become almost invisible. Consequently, characters in ancient writing were often reduced to the role of faceless, formless agents who existed primarily to advance the action

1. This idea appears throughout Aristotle's *Poetics*; see especially chap. 6 for his specific description of how action and character function.

of the story. Apart from Jesus—the only fully developed character in the narrative—most other characters in John's Gospel function in the manner described above. Some characters are developed more than others, but almost every character exists to serve the narrator's agenda, which is to clarify the gospel's exalted Christology. Most characters appear briefly in the story, allowing little room for substantial development. From the outset of the gospel, characters such as John the Baptist (1:26–36), Andrew (1:41), Philip (1:45), and Nathanael (1:49) make an appearance simply to confess something about Jesus in a way that is either consistent with or different from what has been revealed in the Prologue. Though the narrator reports the direct speech and cognitive awareness of these characters, they have little significance beyond their initial appearances. They appear and just as quickly disappear as part of the flotsam and jetsam of the narrative.

The various characters in the gospel approach Jesus with different levels of understanding, but no one—outside of the Beloved Disciple (see table 6.1 below)—approaches him fully comprehending the truths that have been revealed to the reader. It is possible then for the reader to evaluate the correctness of every character's interaction with Jesus. In order to gain a clearer understanding of how characters misunderstand Jesus, we must look at what the reader already knows about him. With this information in mind, it becomes clear to the reader how characters consistently misunderstand what Jesus is saying and also allows the reader to trace a given misunderstanding back to an insight that has been revealed in the Prologue.

As the story moves along, characters are used as a means of further explaining Jesus' message, mission, and identity; this is often accomplished by means of the motif of misunderstanding. Scholars have thoroughly investigated the role misunderstanding plays in the gospel.[2] This motif is important to the overall rhetoric of the narrative and usually occurs in the context of some kind of verbal or situational irony (see the full discussion of this in chapter 5). As discussed in chapter 2, the greatest source of direct information about Jesus is found in the gospel's Prologue. These opening verses detail the origins and divinity of Jesus (1:1–2), his role in creation (1:3), his status as the light of humanity (1:5, 9), his dominion over the created order (1:10–11), his rejection by "his own" (1:11), his incarnation and glory (1:14), and his revealing of the Father (1:18). These themes are woven throughout the gospel in a way that consistently points the reader back to the Prologue. Without that information the reader is destined to grope in the "darkness" that shrouds many of John's characters. This is where our awareness of the misunderstanding motif directly touches upon our experience with the characters of John's Gospel.

The narrator and reader of John's Gospel form an "inside group" that has privileged knowledge about Jesus. The characters in the story are part of an "outside group" that is constantly struggling to come to terms with Jesus' identity and mission. The narrator is omniscient. He knows whom Jesus loves (11:5; 13:1–3, 23; 19:26; 20:2), what Jesus perceives (6:6, 15, 61, 64; 13:1; 19:28), and when Jesus is troubled (11:33, 38; 13:1). He provides information about the beliefs (2:11, 22; 20:8), suppositions (13:19; 20:15), and memories of the disciples (2:22; 12:16; 13:28; 19:35). The narrator guides the reader skillfully through a maze of reported activities, interactions, and conversations. Unlike the narrator, the reader is informed but not omniscient. The reader shares in much of this privileged information with

2. See, e.g., Carson, "Understanding Misunderstandings," 59–91; Richard, "Expressions of Double Meaning," 96–112; Pyle, "Understanding the Misunderstanding Sequences," 26–47.

the narrator but continues to learn throughout the story. By contrast, the characters of the gospel do not have access to this "inside view." (At this point, it may be helpful to refer back to the *Columbo* illustration that was introduced in chapter 2.) This literary dynamic places readers in a position to evaluate every character's response to Jesus. As the story moves forward, characters appear to understand or misunderstand Jesus to the degree that they grasp ideas earlier unveiled in the Prologue. Since no character (except the Beloved Disciple) fully grasps these truths, each expresses some degree of misunderstanding. The narrator then uses Jesus' words to clarify the fuller meaning of these themes. Readers soon discover that numerous character interactions in the gospel follow a predictable pattern:

(1) Jesus speaks/acts in the presence of another character. This activity usually addresses some element of Jesus' mission.
(2) The character in question misperceives some element of Jesus' words or actions. This misunderstanding requires either correction or further instruction.
(3) Jesus speaks again, this time in a way that is intended to clarify what has been misunderstood.
(4) In each instance, one or more themes from the Prologue are raised, revealing the character's misunderstanding, exposing the reader's knowledge once again, and ultimately clarifying the truth about Jesus.

There is not space in this brief chapter for a comprehensive demonstration of how this pattern works with each character in the gospel (for more examples, see Figure 6.2).[3] The remainder of this chapter will attempt to use Peter as a

3. For more on how John's characters function, see Hylen, *Imperfect Believers*; Skinner, *Characters and Characterization in the Gospel of John*.

Table 6.1

The Beloved Disciple—Disciple *Par Excellence*

There is one character in the Gospel of John who consistently gets everything correct—the Beloved Disciple. The shadowy figure known as "the disciple whom Jesus loved," appears in four scenes in the Gospel of John (13:21–30; 18:15–18; 19:26–27; 21:7, 20), though some also regard the unnamed disciple in John 1:35–39 as the Beloved Disciple. In these scenes the Beloved Disciple stands in contrast to Simon Peter, who is characterized less positively. In each instance the Beloved Disciple responds to Jesus in a way that the narrator considers praiseworthy, while Peter expresses confusion, doubt, and misunderstanding, ultimately denying that he knows Jesus. In a sense, the Beloved Disciple gets everything right: twice he is found in a location that indicates his loyalty to Jesus (18:15–18; 19:25–27); he responds appropriately by believing at the empty tomb, even when he does not understand (20:3–8); he also recognizes the risen Jesus from afar while the other disciples do not (21:7). In what is probably the most important comment about the Beloved Disciple, the narrator depicts him as "leaning back on the chest of Jesus" (13:25)—an English rendering of the same Greek phrase used to describe the relationship between Jesus and the Father ("close to the Father's heart"; 1:18 NRSV). Each of these depictions reinforces the idea that the Beloved Disciple should be seen as an ideal follower of Jesus—one with whom any faithful reader can and should identify. The Beloved Disciple is anonymous in the text and must remain so to fulfill the role given him in the story. The point is that any reader who wishes to follow Jesus can become a Beloved Disciple by following his lead. From the pages of the story the Beloved Disciple beckons the reader: "Follow Jesus as I have followed him, and you too can become a disciple whom Jesus loves" (Excerpted from Christopher W. Skinner, "Who Was the Beloved Disciple?," at *Bible Odyssey*: http://www.bibleodyssey.org/people/related-articles/who-was-the-beloved-disciple.aspx.)

test case for the description of characters provided above. Since Peter appears more often and speaks more frequently than any other character, he is a paradigm for our understanding of how John's characters function. This exercise will allow the reader to draw conclusions about character formation to interpret other character interactions in the narrative.

PETER: A TEST CASE

Peter is initially set up to be a sympathetic character in the eyes of the reader, only to descend into serious misunderstanding throughout the rest of the story. Although he is never fully rehabilitated in the story proper, the addition of chapter 21—the so-called Epilogue—provides a full redemption for Peter in the eyes of the reader. We will examine all of the twists and turns of Peter's journey, including his "extreme makeover" in John 21.

1. Peter in John 1:35–42

The audience meets Peter for the first time in 1:35–42 on the day following John's proclamation that Jesus is the "Lamb of God" (1:29) and "God's Chosen One" (1:34). In 1:36 John announces for a second time that Jesus is the "Lamb of God," this time in the presence of two unnamed disciples. Having heard their teacher exalt Jesus three times, two of John's disciples leave him and begin to follow Jesus. After his initial conversation with Jesus (1:38–39), one of the disciples, Andrew, seeks his brother to inform him that they "have found the Messiah" (1:41b). Identifying Andrew by name, the narrator refers to him as the brother of Simon Peter (v. 40a). Little narrative time passes between the first mention of Simon Peter (v. 40) and his first meeting with Jesus (v. 42b). This face-to-face encounter is immediately followed by the changing of

TABLE 6.2

"Representative" Characters in John

The tendency to regard Johannine characters as symbolic of a specific group or a greater spiritual reality has been pervasive in the history of exegesis on the Fourth Gospel. According to this approach, each character possesses one discernible, dominant trait (e.g., belief, unbelief) that highlights one aspect of a proper or improper response to Jesus. In 1976, Raymond F. Collins published his influential, two-part study of 'representative figures' in John. This marked an important development in character studies. According to Collins, characters in the gospel embody a dominant trait that is *intended by the Evangelist* to represent a certain type of faith response to Jesus. These types are further meant to function as models for the audience to emulate or reject based upon the narrative's call to believe and follow Jesus (e.g., 20:31). More recent work on Johannine characterization has identified two inherent weaknesses in the representative approach. First, the model tends to categorize characters in a way that fails to account for the complexity that we find in many Johannine figures. Second, there is a general lack of unanimity among scholars as to what trait the representative figures actually embody. In other words, it has proven difficult to arrive at a consensus on the representative function of each supposedly representative figure. Despite these weaknesses, however, the representative approach has not been completely abandoned in contemporary scholarship on the Gospel of John.

Simon's name. The narrator introduces this new character as Simon Peter after which Jesus proclaims, "You shall be called Cephas," which means "rock" (v. 42d). The rapid pace of these events should be somewhat arresting for the reader, and Jesus' immediate changing of Peter's name is seemingly an announcement of who Peter is and what he will become. This initial interaction between Jesus and Peter is a positive sign for the early development of Peter's character. The reader's initial impression of Peter should be a favorable one.

2. Peter in John 6:60–71

a. Summary: Peter makes his second appearance in 6:68, on the day following Jesus' multiplication of loaves for the five thousand (cf. 6:1–15). John 6 narrates a series of events over a two-day span, which culminates in two mutually exclusive responses to Jesus by his "disciples." At several turns in the so-called "Bread of Life discourse" (6:25–59) Jesus' words have led to confusion and outrage among the crowds. Of particular offense is his insistence that they must "eat his flesh" and "drink his blood" in order to have eternal life (6:54). This saying produces the two opposing responses to Jesus in vv. 60–71. One group falls away on account of this saying and the other draws closer to Jesus. Here, Peter is again presented in a substantially positive light.

b. Examining Peter: In v. 60 "many disciples" react negatively to the difficult saying. A key reason why these disciples fail to grasp and accept what Jesus has said is that they have taken his words about "eating flesh" and "drinking blood" literally (see the discussion of misplaced literalism in chapter 5). So Jesus condemns the flesh as useless and then affirms that his words are not flesh but spirit and life (v. 63). Here the reader is supposed to recall two statements from the Prologue: (1) "in him was *life* and that *life* was the light of humanity" (1:4); and (2) Jesus "became flesh and dwelt among us" (1:14). However, the disciples hearing this message do not have access to these insights and reject Jesus' teaching. Their inability to understand Jesus ultimately gives way to their unbelief, which Jesus confirms in v. 64. They collectively decide that this "hard saying" is ultimately too difficult to accept and they depart in ignorance (v. 66).

Aware that many disciples have left, Jesus now turns to "the Twelve" and asks if they intend to depart as well

TABLE 6.3

Other Examples of Character Misunderstanding in the Gospel of John

2:19–22: Jesus tells the crowds, "Destroy this temple and I will raise it again in three days." They take him literally, but he is referring to the "temple of his body."

3:3–4: Nicodemus mistakenly thinks that Jesus is talking about a literal second birth, but he is actually speaking about being born "from above."

4:10–15: Jesus speaks to the Samaritan woman about "living water" but he is figuratively referring to "water that imparts life." She mistakenly believes he is talking about "running water" and asks her to provide this for her.

4:31–38: Jesus tells his disciples, "I have food that you do not know about." He is speaking figuratively of fulfilling the Father's will, but they believe he is talking about food."

6:43–56: Jesus tells the crowds that they must eat his flesh and drink his blood, which they mistakenly take as a reference to cannibalism. However, he is referring, figuratively, to the practice John's original audience had come to know as the Eucharist.

11:4–16: When discussing Jesus' upcoming trip into Judea, Thomas tells the other disciples, "let us go also that we may die with him," but he fails to realize that Jesus' trip to Judea is about life rather than death. Jesus is intending to raise Lazarus from the dead.

(v. 67). In answer to Jesus' question, Peter confesses, "You have the words of eternal life" (v. 68), recalling the truth of what Jesus has just stated in v. 63 about his words being "spirit and life" and the prominent theme of "belief in Jesus' word" which runs throughout 2:1—4:54.[4] Peter's confession

4. In that unit a handful of characters including the mother of

also affirms truths about Jesus that reflect what the reader has learned in the Prologue. Peter continues to stand out as an example of a character with genuine insights about Jesus. However, his next few appearances will reveal the limitations of those insights.

3. Peter in John 13:1–17

a. Summary: In an example that prefigures his "service" on the cross, Jesus serves his disciples by washing their feet at the beginning of John 13. This is where the reader begins to see Peter's limitations much more clearly as a series of critical misunderstandings ensues. Following the foot-washing, the disciples and Jesus share a meal, at which time Jesus predicts that he will be betrayed by one of the Twelve. When Jesus informs the disciples that he is going away and that they will be unable to follow, Peter protests that he is willing to lay down his own life for Jesus. This naïve announcement is met with Jesus' correction and a prediction of Peter's future threefold denial.

b. Examining Peter: In 13:1–5, Jesus is washing and drying the disciples' feet until he comes to Peter, at which point there is an abrupt break in the foot-washing. Peter first expresses surprise and then registers an outright objection ("You will never wash my feet!" v. 6). The Greek construction used here (*ou mē* plus the aorist subjunctive)

Jesus (2:5), the Samaritans (4:39), and the royal official (4:50) believe Jesus on the basis of his word. By contrast Nicodemus (3:4, 9) fails to believe because he does not understand Jesus' words. At this stage of the narrative, Peter fits squarely within the tradition of those who believe in Jesus' word. Peter also proclaims that Jesus is the "Holy One of God" (6:69). With these words the audience witnesses another confession to add to the growing list of christological affirmations in the gospel.

underscores the intensity of Peter's protest. This construction is the strongest way to negate something in Hellenistic Greek, denying even the potentiality of an action. In response to Peter's protest, Jesus declares that if Peter rejects the foot-washing he can have no share (Greek: *meros*) with

Table 6.4

Named v. Anonymous Characters in John

The Gospel of John, displays remarkable precision in identifying characters in the Fourth Gospel by name, birthplace, parentage, etc. In addition, the narrator meticulously identifies places, defines Semitic terms, and possesses knowledge of events beyond the scope of any character in the narrative. Therefore, it is interesting to note the numerous instances where concern for detail is conspicuous by its absence—specifically the nameless, faceless, but literarily significant characters in John's story. Often in narrative literature anonymous characters are merely agents who help guide the action of the story. We see this especially in the Synoptic Gospels where the absence of a name is often an indicator of unimportance. However, in John, those who might otherwise be regarded as unimportant become models of faith and stand out in stark contrast to those who are named directly. The mother of Jesus is a poignant example of this. Though she is anonymous she ultimately becomes paradigmatic for belief—the gospel's central theological emphasis. We see this importance in the anonymous Samaritan woman who unwittingly evangelizes her entire village and becomes the first witness to Jesus. To illustrate this further, we turn to Jesus' arrest in the garden. Is it reasonable to conclude that the name of Jesus' mother was unknown or unimportant to an author who took the time to record the name of an agent such as Malchus, the servant whose ear was cut off at Jesus' arrest (18:10)? There is some greater literary or theological significance in John's use of anonymity; this suggests that anonymous characters are an important part of the gospel's approach to characterization. For more on this, see Watty, "The Significance of Anonymity in the Fourth Gospel."

Jesus. Often translated "part," the term likely refers to a portion of an inheritance—a concept upon which Jesus will elaborate in 14:2–3. Once again, Peter does not understand what Jesus means and responds by asking Jesus to wash his feet, head, and hands. In a manner similar to the rigidly literal crowds in John 6, Peter fails to see the symbolism in the washing of his feet. He is focused on the act itself. If the act of washing brings one into union with Jesus, Peter wants more than a foot-washing; he desires that his entire body be cleansed. The reader cannot question Peter's sincerity, but is beginning to have doubts about whether he truly understands Jesus.

4. Peter in John 13:18–38

a. Summary: After the foot-washing is complete, Jesus begins to be troubled in spirit and informs the Twelve that one among them—the one who was previously called a "devil"—will betray him (13:18–22). Upon hearing this statement the disciples begin speculating as to who the betrayer might be. In v. 23 the audience meets the "disciple whom Jesus loved" for the first time. From this point forward, when the reader encounters Peter, the Beloved Disciple is usually present.[5] Here the Beloved Disciple is seated next to Jesus and leaning against his breast (Greek: *en tō kolpō*)—a description that in Greek recalls the portrayal of Jesus in the Prologue ("close to the Father's heart"; Greek: *eis ton kolpon*; 1:18). This description sets up an implicit contrast between the Beloved Disciple, who is experiencing an intimate union

5. The only time they are separated throughout the remainder of the gospel is in chs. 18–19. A critical contrast is set up between Peter (ch. 18) who denies Jesus, and the Beloved Disciple (ch. 19), the only member of the Twelve to draw near to Jesus' cross. They are together at the empty tomb and they are together in ch. 21. Some believe the "other disciple" in 18:15 should be understood as the Beloved Disciple.

with Jesus like the one Jesus displays with the Father, and Peter who descends into greater misunderstanding.

b. Examining Peter: Filled with curiosity about the betrayer, Peter asks the Beloved Disciple to play the role of intermediary and find out the identity of the person about whom Jesus is speaking. The Beloved Disciple asks (v. 25) and Jesus answers (v. 26) but curiously the Beloved Disciple never reports the answer to Peter. The reader, however, knows that Judas Iscariot is the betrayer, and by receiving the dipped morsel, Judas confirms this role. In accord with Jesus' command (v. 27) Judas departs immediately (v. 30).

On the heels of Judas's departure Jesus begins to explain his "glorification." He has spoken of his glory on a number of previous occasions in the narrative.[6] In this setting he speaks of his glorification in the context of his betrayal and death. The hour (Greek: *hōra*) for which the audience has been waiting has finally arrived.[7] Jesus tells the disciples that he will be going away and they will not be able to join him (13:33; cf. 7:33). Again Peter's ignorance is front and center when he asks Jesus, "Where are you going?" (v. 36a). The reader knows that Jesus is from the Father (1:1–2) and here learns that Jesus will return to the Father through his crucifixion. Peter is unaware of Jesus' heavenly origins and therefore fails to appreciate what it means for Jesus to return, even if through the violent means of the cross.

6. The theme was introduced in the Prologue in 1:14. The audience sees Jesus "reveal his glory" in 2:11. Then, in 8:50, 54; 11:4, 40; 14:13; 16:14; 17:4, 5, 10, 22, 24, Jesus speaks of the glory he and the Father share that will ultimately be revealed in his betrayal, crucifixion, and resurrection.

7. Jesus has previously spoken about his "hour" in 2:4; 4:21, 23; 5:25, 28; 7:30; 8:20; 12:23, 27.

Jesus refuses to answer and reinforces what he has earlier said in v. 33—the disciples cannot come to where he is going. His hour has come and his glorification entails a departure to the Father who sent him. Because Peter does not understand this truth, he ignorantly protests that he is willing to lay down his life for Jesus. His insistence is met with Jesus' sarcastic question ("Will you *really* lay down your life for me?") and an authoritative contradiction ("Amen, amen I say to you, before the rooster crows you will deny me three times"; v. 38). The reader is arrested by the prediction of Peter's denials. While Peter may fall short of fully comprehending the truth of Jesus' origins and identity, he has been a positive and sympathetic character up to this point in the story. At this point it is difficult to imagine him denying Jesus. Nevertheless, his numerous misunderstandings have put him on an increasingly negative trajectory that will not be reversed until John 21.

5. Peter in John 18:1–14

a. Summary: At the conclusion of the Farewell Discourse, Jesus and the disciples have departed across the Kidron Valley (18:1). In an unnamed garden the events of Jesus' final night and day begin to unfold. Judas Iscariot, earlier dispatched to complete his commission "quickly" (13:27), leads Roman soldiers and a detachment from the chief priests and Pharisees to arrest Jesus in the garden. After a brief conversation in which Jesus self-identifies twice as the "I am" (cf. vv. 5, 6, 8; see also the discussion of "I am" statements in chapter 5), he is taken to the Jewish authorities. While Jesus is inside facing the Jewish leaders, Peter is outside denying that he knows Jesus. The predictions of betrayal from John 13 are now realized.

b. Examining Peter: Jesus and the disciples have now ventured out into a garden where the earlier prediction of betrayal by one of Jesus' closest friends is coming to pass. Judas appears accompanied by an unlikely pairing of groups. With him are a Roman cohort[8] and a delegation of temple officers sent from the chief priests and Pharisees. In v. 5, the narrator indicates that Judas is "with them," a subtle but damning description. Judas's loyalties now lie with Jesus' opponents. Opposition to Jesus makes for strange bedfellows as he is now face-to-face with one of his disciples (Judas), the Jewish leaders (with whom he has been at odds throughout the entire gospel), and members of a new group (representatives of the Roman government).

Peter and the other disciples are granted release from the imminent police action of the mob, though Peter's actions in v. 10 reveal once again a fundamental misunderstanding of Jesus' mission. If Jesus is going to return to the Father, he must be arrested by this delegation of temple police and soldiers. This is the way to the cross, which for John's Jesus is the way back to the Father. Instead of departing, however, Peter pulls his sword and strikes Malchus, the servant of the high priest, cutting off his right ear. Jesus rebukes Peter for his impetuous action by commanding him to put his sword away, and by pointing out that he must fulfill the will of the Father (v. 11). Jesus' question to Peter—"Shall I not drink the cup the Father has given to me?"—is the climactic moment in this scene and, as in previous scenes, there is neither a response from Peter nor an explanation by the narrator. The setting shifts without a word about Peter's misunderstanding. The reader needs no explanation; the narrator intends this silence as an implicit criticism of Peter's inability to see the divinely-prescribed destiny of Jesus.

8. A Roman cohort was a military unit with a capacity of 600 soldiers.

6. Peter in John 18:15–27:

a. Summary: As the mob leaves the garden, Jesus is bound, taken into custody, and brought before the Jewish leadership. While Jesus is inside being questioned by Annas, Peter is outside being questioned by those who are standing around and warming themselves. A critical contrast develops between the actions of Jesus and Peter. Jesus speaks boldly before those who have authority to condemn him, while Peter cowers in the presence of a little girl and a slave (18:17, 26). Jesus confesses the truth, while Peter denies it, consequently disavowing Jesus. Even the prior confession of Jesus ("I am"; Greek: *egō eimi*; vv. 5b, 6b, 8a) stands in contrast to Peter's denials ("I am not"; Greek: *ouk eimi*; vv. 17, 25).

b. Examining Peter: While Jesus is inside being questioned by Annas, Simon Peter and "another disciple" are following at a distance. The other disciple is acquainted with the high priest and is able to gain access to the courtyard (v. 15). Eventually Peter (v. 16) gains access to the inside when the other disciple speaks to a slave girl who watches the door and Peter is allowed to enter. The introduction of this slave girl provides Peter his first opportunity to confess or deny Jesus. As he enters the courtyard, the slave girl inquires of him, "You are not one of the disciples of this man, are you?" The Greek construction indicates that her question expects a negative answer and that is exactly what Peter provides. By replying, "I am not" (Greek: *ouk eimi*; v. 17b), Peter not only denies Jesus but also utters words that stand out against the threefold appearance of "I am" (Greek: *egō eimi*) in vv. 5–8.

This scene ends with a side comment from the narrator. A group of characters, including slaves and guards, are warming themselves by the fire in the courtyard of the high priest (v. 18a). The narrator comments that Peter is "with them" (v. 18b), a phrase which recalls the earlier presence of Judas among the members of the arresting party ("Judas, the one who betrayed him, was with them"; v. 5). This connection between the betrayals of Judas and Peter that was so vividly drawn in John 13 is reemphasized here in this scene. The irony is that, while Jesus is inside facing the judgment by the Jewish leaders, Peter is outside in subtle, if unintentional, collusion with those who oppose Jesus. Even when Peter is on the inside (in the courtyard with the other disciple), he remains an outsider because he is "with them."

The setting briefly flashes back to Jesus' interview before Annas (vv. 19–24) before returning to Peter who is still "with them." While being questioned, Jesus responds to Annas, "Ask those who have heard me" (v. 22). Ironically, this could be accomplished by going out and questioning Peter! Meanwhile, an unidentified group within the courtyard asks Peter for a second time whether he is one of Jesus' disciples. As with his first denial, the question posed to Peter expects a negative answer, which he again provides: "I am not" (Greek: *ouk eimi*; v. 25). Without a break in the action Peter is questioned for a third time about his relationship to Jesus. This time a relative of Malchus (18:10) poses the question and the Greek construction betrays the expectation of an affirmative answer (v. 26). The question recalls Peter's presence with those in the courtyard and again draws the intended contrast. Will Peter confess to having been "with him" or will he deny it and remain "with them?" Having heard Jesus' prediction in John 13, the reader is not surprised that Peter denies knowing Jesus for a third time. After the third denial the rooster crows immediately. In denying Jesus, Peter has failed to honor the love commandment and has become a betrayer on the level of Judas Iscariot.

7. Peter in John 20:1–10

a. Summary: The last time the reader saw Peter was on the occasion of his third denial (18:26–27) and his final words in the text were words of disavowal ("I am not," 18:25). Since then there has been no mention of Peter and no attempt to absolve him of the responsibility of denying Jesus three times. Nevertheless, Peter retains the important status he has achieved throughout the gospel. This much is clear in the depiction of Mary's discovery of the empty tomb. Peter becomes the first recipient of the news (v. 2) and despite his recent indiscretions, he remains chief among the small group of Jesus-followers.

b. Examining Peter: It is now early on the first day of the week. The narrator makes sure to point out that these events take place "while it was still dark" (v. 1a). The reader recognizes the theological motif of "darkness" and its association with unbelief throughout the gospel.[9] Again, the audience is led back to the words of the Prologue: "The light shines in the darkness and the darkness has not overcome it" (1:5). The light of the world has seemingly been extinguished by the proceedings of the previous few days, but the events at the empty tomb will confirm that the light has triumphed over darkness.

Mary Magdalene, whom the reader has only just met at the foot of the cross in 19:25, is the first to venture to the tomb of Jesus.[10] Upon arriving she notices that the stone

9. Cf., e.g., 1:5; 3:2; 6:17; 9:4; 8:12; 11:10; 12:35, 46; 13:30; 19:39.

10. Mary appears in the passion and resurrection narratives of all three Synoptics (Mark 15:40, 47; 16:1; Matt 27:56, 61; 28:1; Luke 24:10). She also appears earlier in Luke's Gospel (8:2), where it is reported that Jesus cast seven demons out of her. Mary Magdalene is not a prominent figure in the Fourth Gospel. However, in light of her appearance in the synoptic resurrection traditions, it is unlikely that

has been rolled away from the entrance. Mary's immediate response is not to investigate the tomb but rather to run directly to the disciples. She finds Simon Peter and the Beloved Disciple and reports that the tomb is empty (v. 2). Her report leads to immediate action on the part of the two disciples.

In vv. 3–4 the two disciples depart *toward* the tomb, and as they make their way they are running together. The picture of the two disciples in vv. 3–4 contrasts with the description of Mary Magdalene who in v. 2 ran away from the tomb. As the two disciples are running, the Beloved Disciple passes Peter and arrives first. The reader already perceives the Beloved Disciple's position as the disciple *par excellence* in the Fourth Gospel (cf. 13:23–26; 19:25–27). Throughout the gospel the reader has also seen Peter in a position of leadership over the disciples—though his example has not always been exemplary. In this instance, however, both disciples run away from the situation of darkness and "unfaith" evident in Mary's words and depart toward the tomb, the place of faith associated with God's intervention in the story. The Beloved Disciple is the first of Jesus' disciples to witness the linen cloths lying inside the empty tomb. He observes the tomb but cautiously stops short of entering (v. 5); by contrast Peter reaches the tomb second and immediately enters (v. 6).

The description of what Peter sees in the tomb is much more detailed than what the Beloved Disciple witnesses. The latter simply sees "the strips of linen cloth there" (v. 5); Peter, on the other hand, sees "the strips of linen cloth there" (v. 6b), "the towel which had been upon his head" (v. 7a), and notices that "it was not with the strips of linen cloth but rolled up in a place by itself" (v. 7b). Despite this information, the narrator does not comment on Peter's

she was unknown to the original readership of John.

response to what he has witnessed, though the audience is explicitly told that the Beloved Disciple "saw and believed," (v. 8). It is hard to miss the contrasts created by this presentation of the two disciples. While both disciples move toward genuine faith, the narrator continues to elevate the Beloved Disciple. Both see the empty tomb (vv. 6–8); both fail to understand the Scripture indicating that Jesus must rise from the dead (v. 9); only the Beloved Disciple is said to believe.

While both disciples are moving in the direction of faith, the narrator persists in providing a picture of the Beloved Disciple as the disciple *par excellence*. Peter is shown moving from darkness toward light and from unfaith toward faith, but he will not fully learn what the audience knows until he comes face-to-face with the risen Jesus.

In his previous two appearances, Peter had failed to understand Jesus' symbolic actions (the foot-washing, 13:1–20), explicit teaching about his departure (13:24–38), nonresistance to his departure (18:10–11), or the importance of laying down one's life as implied by the love command (18:15–18, 25–27; cf. 13:34–35). Nevertheless, when he along with the Beloved Disciple hears the report of the empty tomb he responds by moving toward the location of God's entrance into the story (20:3–10). In this unit Peter regains some of his luster of early appearances and is on his way toward becoming the "Rock" alluded to in 1:42. He shows a level of trust and spiritual comprehension, but he has not yet been fully restored in the eyes of the implied audience.

8. Peter in John 21:1–14

a. Summary: Most scholars working on the Gospel of John acknowledge that John 21 is likely a later addition to the original text. Although there are no manuscripts in which chapter 21 is missing, most feel that 20:31 is the original ending and that ch. 21 was added to vindicate Peter in the eyes of later readers; this creates something of a problem for our evaluation of Peter and for the narration of events as a whole. Apart from ch. 21, Peter never fully realizes the promise of Jesus in 1:42, while in John 21 there is a concerted effort to restore Peter to his status as the "rock" for the early post-resurrection church.

b. Examining Peter: The narrator begins by providing details of Jesus' third post-resurrection appearance to the disciples. This appearance occurs in the context of fishing. Peter, Thomas, and Nathanael (all of whom the reader has met previously), the sons of Zebedee (who are not mentioned in the Fourth Gospel to this point) and two unnamed disciples are together in Galilee. Peter decides to go fishing and the others join him (v. 3). The reader learns in v. 3c that their fishing expedition is a failure. The disciples catch nothing, failing in their endeavor until Jesus comes to assist. After his arrival on the shore they pull in 153 fish (v. 11).

Jesus stands on the shore and calls out to the disciples but they do not recognize him. They have been unsuccessful in their fishing, but after a strange directive from Jesus (v. 6a), the disciples begin to haul in a massive catch (v. 6b). Instantly the Beloved Disciple recognizes Jesus and tells Peter "it is the Lord" (Greek: *kyrios estin*; v. 7a). Again the Beloved Disciple is elevated at Peter's expense. He is the first to recognize Jesus and identify him as "Lord." At this statement, Peter plunges into the water and swims for the shore (v. 8) while the others bring the boat back to the shore. Peter's action of jumping into the water without waiting for the boat to return to land is an initial indication of his restoration by the narrator. The previous picture of the Beloved Disciple passing Peter on the way to the tomb (20:3–4) suggested that the Beloved Disciple had a greater love for Jesus than did Peter. Here, while the greater insight still belongs to the Beloved Disciple ("it is the Lord," v. 7), the greater zeal for Jesus clearly belongs to Peter. As Peter swims, the disciples redirect the boat and head for shore. All the while they are dragging the net full of fish (v. 8).

When the disciples arrive, they find that Jesus has prepared a breakfast of fish and bread (v. 9). He instructs the disciples to bring some of the fish they have just caught (v. 10). Notably, of all the disciples present, it is Peter who pulls the net ashore (v. 11). Again, Peter's actions are a signal to the reader of his faith. They are also to be regarded as a symbolic statement on Peter's role of leadership in the early church—a role that will be spelled out in greater detail in the following section.

9. Peter in John 21:15–23

a. Summary: In this unit, the reader witnesses the restoration of Peter in a threefold reversal that is meant to recall Peter's three denials in 18:15–17, 25–27. Jesus asks Peter three separate times, "Do you love me?" In each instance Peter affirms his love. While it is lost on Peter, the reader is supposed to catch the clear link between Peter's three previous denials and his three new opportunities to profess his love for Jesus. The coward of ch. 18 is becoming the "rock" of the church. Whereas the end of the gospel offered no sweeping image enhancement for Peter, ch. 21 moves toward Peter's full restoration in this conversation with the risen Jesus. In addition to the three questions by Jesus and professions by Peter, there are also three commands for Peter to take care of Jesus' sheep. Peter is not only being restored, he is also being given a position of leadership in the early church.

b. Examining Peter: In v. 15, the group has finished eating and Jesus turns to Peter (here identified as Simon Peter) and asks, "Simon son of John, do you love me more than these?" This begins a sequence of three question-and-answer episodes between Jesus and Peter. These brief episodes run as follows:

	21:15	**21:16**	**21:17**
Jesus asks:	"Simon son of John, do you love me more than these?"	"Simon son of John, do you love me?"	"Simon son of John, do you love me?"
Peter answers:	"Yes Lord. You know that I love you."	"Yes Lord. You know that I love you."	"Lord, you know all things. You know that I love you."
Jesus commands:	"Feed my lambs."	"Tend my sheep."	"Feed my sheep."

Jesus ends this symbolic reinstatement by uttering cryptic words about Peter being bound and led away by others (v. 18). In an aside, the reader learns in v. 19 that this statement is meant by Jesus to indicate the manner of Peter's death. After this brief exchange with Peter, Jesus utters two important words "follow me" (v. 19). The command leads to another exchange between Peter and Jesus. For now, the manner of Peter's death is ancillary. The mission Peter is given necessitates that he follow Jesus.

During the conversation with Jesus, Peter turns and notices the Beloved Disciple and asks Jesus, "What about him?" (v. 21), to which Jesus responds, "If I want him to remain until I return, what is that to you?" (v. 22b).

Within the story, Jesus' reply is meant to distinguish clearly for the early readers the roles of Peter and the Beloved Disciple. Jesus has just given to Peter (the "rock") the role of shepherd (i.e., leader) of the church. Peter's question advances the argument of the appendix and provides the Johannine Jesus an opportunity to clarify the role of the Beloved Disciple. Each disciple has a prominent role. Peter is the leader while the Beloved Disciple is the enduring witness. In the end, the supreme role still belongs to the Beloved Disciple. Peter is restored but the Beloved Disciple remains the Johannine hero.

Conclusion: A Mixed Portrait: When the entire presentation of Peter in the Gospel of John has been considered, a mixed portrait emerges. He begins with a promise that never fully materializes according to the expectations developed by the reader. Nevertheless, Peter retains a fixed importance in the gospel and is eventually restored in ch. 21. In John 13, 18, and 20 the trait most consistently demonstrated by Peter is a failure to understand Jesus and to respond properly to him. However, in John 21 he is vindicated, though he remains a notch below the Beloved Disciple.

PETER AS PARADIGM

The extended consideration of Simon Peter in this chapter is intended to help validate the theory that character misunderstanding is a major part of the narrator's rhetorical strategy and is related both to the Prologue's description of Jesus and the gospel's overall christological presentation. We see that Peter's misunderstandings reveal his ignorance about concepts to which the reader has already been exposed in John 1:1–18. Throughout the story, the audience must continually return to the information revealed in the

Prologue in order to evaluate character responses to Jesus along with other elements of the narrative. Uncomprehending characters advance the plot by causing the audience to look back at what has been revealed, which in turn points forward to the cumulative effect of the story to that point. In each instance of misunderstanding the reader is reminded of both the information already given about Jesus and how each character in the story has received him thus far. This constant back-and-forth movement helps contribute to the narrator's desired effect by keeping the reader aware of what has transpired and building anticipation for what will take place as the story moves toward its climax. In this way, John's misunderstanding characters advance the action of the story while emphasizing the gospel's Christology.

John's misunderstanding characters also help clarify the presentation of several interwoven theological themes in the gospel. The identity of Jesus is laid out in the Prologue and a proper or improper understanding of Jesus' identity has implications for the reader's view of belief, Christology, and the Johannine theology of the cross. These related themes come to the forefront of the narrative every time an uncomprehending character fails to understand Jesus. An understanding of Jesus' identity informs the gospel's christological presentation. An understanding of John's Christology clarifies Jesus' mission toward the cross, which in turn clarifies the nature of authentic belief. Whether explicit or implicit, these themes are present in the reader's encounter with every uncomprehending character. By using the Prologue in concert with misunderstanding characters, the narrator illustrates improper belief in Jesus and beckons the reader to respond by believing (cf. 20:31) from a fully informed perspective.

REFLECTION:

1. Why do you think the author of John's Gospel has intentionally cast characters as unable to understand Jesus? What literary or theological purpose(s) would this have served?

2. This chapter argued that John's characters form an "outside group" that does not share the same knowledge as the "inside group" made up of the narrator and reader. How does understanding John's characters as an "outside group" help you to better appreciate their literary purpose?

Chapter 7

PUTTING THE PIECES TOGETHER

READING JOHN 3:1–21

In this final chapter we will pull together elements from the previous chapters and attempt to read a specific passage from the Gospel of John using the reading strategy we have developed. The goal of reading a small piece of the narrative is to incorporate as much of the foregoing material as possible, put the various narrative pieces together, and demonstrate how to read the Gospel of John as a coherent and autonomous story. Here we will look at one of the more well-known passages in the Gospel of John—Jesus' conversation with Nicodemus in 3:1–21. The episode can be divided into two units, the first of which consists of a three-part exchange between Jesus and a new character named Nicodemus, and the second of which is an explanation of Jesus' words as they relate to his mission.

The first twelve verses can be subdivided into three units, each beginning with a statement or question from Nicodemus followed by an explanation from Jesus. Nicodemus speaks in vv. 2, 4, and 9 and Jesus responds with a double amen statement in vv. 3, 5, and 11. The conversation (vv. 1–12) is then followed by a brief explanation from Jesus (vv. 13–15) and an extended theological explanation from the narrator (vv. 16–21).[1]

The following outline provides the structure of this passage:

I. Nicodemus and Jesus Converse (3:1–12)

- A. Introduction of Nicodemus (vv. 1–2a)
- B. Conversation, Part 1 (vv. 2b–3)
- C. Conversation, Part 2 (vv. 4–8)
- D. Conversation, Part 3 (vv. 9–12)

II. Explaining Jesus' Words (3:13–21)

- A. Jesus Clarifies His Teaching (vv. 13–15)
- B. The Narrator Clarifies Jesus' Teaching (vv. 16–21)

I. Nicodemus and Jesus Converse (3:1–12)

As the reader approaches John 3, many questions about Jesus have been answered, though many still remain. The reader knows that Jesus is the unique representation of God (1:1c) and the revealer of the Father to humanity (1:18), but these truths are still playing out in the story. In ch. 2, Jesus began his public ministry with a unique sign—turning water into wine (2:1–11)—and an authenticating act in the temple (2:12–22). As ch. 3 begins the reader is led directly into Jesus' conversation with Nicodemus, which represents the first extended dialogue between Jesus and a member of "the Jews" (Greek: *hoi Ioudaioi*) in the narrative.

1. There is debate about where the words of Jesus end and where the explanation of the narrator begins in John 3. This debate is reflected in the commentary tradition as well as in modern translations. The NRSV, NIV, NASB, NLT, and ESV retain quotation marks (or red letters) throughout vv. 16–21, indicating that Jesus' words continue. Alternatively, the NAB and NET place quotation marks at v. 15 and leave vv. 16–21 as plain text. Of the two positions I find the latter more convincing.

Table 7.1
John 3:1–21 (NRSV)

1 Now there was a Pharisee named Nicodemus, a leader of the Jews.
2 He came to Jesus by night and said to him, "Rabbi, we know that
you are a teacher who has come from God; for no one can do these
signs that you do apart from the presence of God." 3 Jesus answered
him, "Very truly, I tell you, no one can see the kingdom of God without being born from above." 4 Nicodemus said to him, "How can
anyone be born after having grown old? Can one enter a second
time into the mother's womb and be born?" 5 Jesus answered, "Very
truly, I tell you, no one can enter the kingdom of God without being
born of water and Spirit. 6 What is born of the flesh is flesh, and
what is born of the Spirit is spirit. 7 Do not be astonished that I said
to you, 'You must be born from above.' 8 The wind blows where it
chooses, and you hear the sound of it, but you do not know where it
comes from or where it goes. So it is with everyone who is born of
the Spirit." 9 Nicodemus said to him, "How can these things be?" 10
Jesus answered him, "Are you a teacher of Israel, and yet you do not
understand these things? 11 "Very truly, I tell you, we speak of what
we know and testify to what we have seen; yet you do not receive
our testimony. 12 If I have told you about earthly things and you do
not believe, how can you believe if I tell you about heavenly things?
13 No one has ascended into heaven except the one who descended
from heaven, the Son of Man. 14 And just as Moses lifted up the
serpent in the wilderness, so must the Son of Man be lifted up, 15
that whoever believes in him may have eternal life." 16 For God so
loved the world that he gave his only Son, so that everyone who believes in him may not perish but may have eternal life. 17 Indeed,
God did not send the Son into the world to condemn the world, but
in order that the world might be saved through him. 18 Those who
believe in him are not condemned; but those who do not believe are
condemned already, because they have not believed in the name of
the only Son of God. 19 And this is the judgment, that the light has
come into the world, and people loved darkness rather than light
because their deeds were evil. 20 For all who do evil hate the light
and do not come to the light, so that their deeds may not be exposed.
21 But those who do what is true come to the light, so that it may be
clearly seen that their deeds have been done in God.

Recalling a number of themes from the Prologue, this conversation provides the narrator an opportunity to explain Jesus' mission further to the reader. Touching on earlier themes of spiritual birth (1:3–6), life (vv. 15, 16), the world (1:16–17), belief (1:16, 18), and light (1:19–21), Jesus' dialogue with Nicodemus (vv. 1–15) and the explanation that follows (vv. 16–21) provide the reader with a clear statement of his mission.

A. Nicodemus Is Introduced (vv. 1–2a). At the close of ch. 2, the events were unfolding in Jerusalem during the time of the Jewish Passover. Since there has been no stated change in setting from 2:23 to 3:1, it is safe to conclude that the events of ch. 3 are also taking place in Jerusalem around the time of the Passover. This episode begins with the introduction of a new character. In v. 1 four crucial pieces of information are given to the reader about this figure: (1) he is a *man*, (2) he is a *Pharisee*, (3) his name is *Nicodemus*, and (4) he is a *religious leader*. Let's look briefly at each of these:

(1) While the term "man" (Greek: *anthrōpos*) can be used to refer to a person irrespective of gender (i.e., "human"), there is a specific reason for the narrator's identification of Nicodemus as "a man." In 2:25, the verse just prior to 3:1, the narrator commented that Jesus needed no testimony concerning man (Greek: *peri tou anthrōpou*) because he knew what was in man (*en tō anthrōpō*). Thus, the narrator's first piece of information is a subtle sign to the reader that Jesus will not entrust himself fully to Nicodemus (see 2:24).

(2) While the name "Nicodemus" does not appear to have a special meaning or significance for the story, it is important that his name is provided at all. In our previous discussion of characters, we saw how differently John treats anonymous characters compared to

those characters whose names are given. By and large, characters that remain nameless in John are presented as models of greater faith than those characters whose names are given. This will prove to be the case here in John 3 where a critical contrast is created with the unnamed Samaritan woman in John 4. Here Nicodemus will walk away from Jesus utterly bewildered while the Samaritan woman will depart with reluctant faith and unwittingly evangelize her entire village (see 4:28–30; 39–42).

(3) At this stage of the story it is difficult to discern the significance of Nicodemus being "from the Pharisees." While some would argue that the Pharisees are characterized throughout the gospel as antagonistic toward Jesus, the reader does not yet know enough of the Pharisees to be suspicious. Though the term will go on to carry hostile overtones throughout the remainder of the story—as is clear in John 7, 9, and 11—that is hardly the case at this early stage of the story. The Pharisees have appeared only once prior to Jesus' conversation with Nicodemus, and that was in the context of questioning John the Baptist (see 1:24). At this stage of the story the reader's mind is not made up about the nature and significance of the Pharisees, though a mostly negative impression will emerge as the story moves forward.

(4) The phrase "ruler of the Jews" is significant on a number of levels. First, it identifies Nicodemus as a member of the Sanhedrin, the Jewish ruling council. This information is meant to set Nicodemus apart as one with strong religious and social credentials. Second, the term "ruler" (Greek: *archē*) is used in John only of the Jewish leaders (see 7:26, 48; 12:42) and Satan, the "ruler of this world" (see 12:31; 14:30; 16:11). So as

the story unfolds the reader begins to grasp the subtle connection between the Jewish leaders and Satan.

At first blush then, an early reader of John's Gospel would likely have found Nicodemus to be a sympathetic character. He is a male member of a respected religious sect as well as part of the Jewish ruling council. Since the reader is not far enough into the story to be overly suspicious of these credentials, Nicodemus will begin his journey in a positive light in the eyes of the reader. However, we must keep in mind that the narrator has already created tension by suggesting that Jesus will not entrust himself to this "man."

In v. 2a the reader learns that Nicodemus has come to Jesus by night (Greek: *pros nuktos*). This detail likely has symbolic significance as a supposedly "enlightened" religious leader seeks Jesus, the "light of the world" after it is dark. As the conversation progresses, the reader will more clearly recognize that Nicodemus's coming by night represents his darkened understanding. Within the story world, this detail may also indicate Nicodemus's unwillingness to make public his interest in Jesus. This means that there is an element of deliberate secrecy on the part of Nicodemus; his attraction to Jesus is at odds with his status in society.

B. Conversation, Part I (vv. 2b–3). The first words Nicodemus utters in the conversation appear to be perceptive though he will rapidly descend into confusion from there. He begins by addressing Jesus with the honorific term "rabbi" and confessing "we know that you are a teacher from God" (v. 2b). The plural likely indicates Nicodemus's status as an official representative of Jewish leadership. More important, however, is the recognition, in line with the Prologue, that Jesus is "from God." This portion of the confession is true from the perspective of the Prologue, but incomplete. The remainder of the dialogue will reveal that Nicodemus's words fall far short of a satisfactory understanding of Jesus' identity.

Nicodemus continues: "We know that no one is able to do the signs you do unless he is from God" (v. 2c). Though he correctly notes for a second time that Jesus is "from God," his understanding of this truth is rooted in a signs-faith, which throughout the Gospel proves to be an inadequate basis for authentic belief. Nicodemus never identifies Jesus as anything more than a miracle-working teacher from God, and while this is partially true, it again falls far short of the understanding of Jesus set forth in the Prologue. What initially seems like a genuine insight is instead a theological perspective from within Nicodemus's first-century Jewish context.

Verse 3 contains Jesus' enigmatic answer to Nicodemus's first statement: "Amen, amen I say to you, unless a person is *born from above*, he will not be able to see the

Table 7.2

The Basis for Authentic Belief: Word v. Works?

Throughout the Gospel of John there is a distinction between those who come to follow Jesus as a result of specific signs they have witnessed, and those who follow on the basis of Jesus' word. Those who believe because of Jesus' works either fall away or show that they do not fully understand Jesus' message, mission, and identity (see Nicodemus in 3:1–12; the crowds in ch. 6). On the other hand, those who act on or believe in Jesus' word are the ultimate models of belief and faithfulness (see e.g., the mother of Jesus in 2:1–11; the woman of Samaria in 4:39–42). This emphasis is perhaps best seen in Jesus' climactic announcement to Thomas in 20:29: "You believe because you have seen [= belief by works]. Blessed are those who have not seen and yet believe [= belief by the proclaimed word].

kingdom of God." For the implied reader this statement stands out as a transparent example of John's *double entendre*. Significant debate centers on the reader's understanding of the Greek phrase *gennēthē anōthen*—often rendered "born again" in English translations. How should the second term in this Greek phrase be understood? A common conclusion among commentators has been that there is a basic misunderstanding on the part of Nicodemus, and this misunderstanding is rooted in the different nuances of the adverb *anōthen*. The standard lexicon used by students of New Testament Greek lists *anōthen* as "an adverb of place," and provides the following definitions:

(1) in extension fr[om] a source that is above, *from above*.

(2) from a point of time marking the beginning of someth[ing], *from the beginning*.

(3) for a relatively long period in the past, *for a long time*.

(4) at a subsequent point of time involving repetition, *again, anew*.[2]

TABLE 7.3

Nicodemus Misunderstands Jesus

Jesus speaks on a higher, spiritual plane
anōthen = "born from above" = spiritual rebirth

Nicodemus interprets on a lower, literal plane
anōthen = "born again" = literal rebirth

Thus, the primary meaning of *anōthen* is "from above" while "again" is an acceptable, though less common nuance. In v. 3, Nicodemus appears to understand Jesus as

2. Danker et al., *Greek-English Lexicon*, 92.

describing an experience of being "born again," though we should probably read the phrase as "born from above." This phenomenon of misunderstanding is in keeping with what we have already discussed in chapter 5. Jesus is speaking on a spiritual plane, while Nicodemus is in error because he has understood Jesus literally. In other words, Nicodemus fails to understand the intended nuance because of a misplaced literalism. His misinterpretation is confirmed by his question in v. 4.[3]

In his commentary, Moloney agrees with the distinction between "from above" and "again," though he offers a middle ground, translating the phrase as "re-birth from above."[4] In support of this suggestion he argues that "the temporal and spatial dimensions of the word are called for by its expansion into 'of water (again) and the Spirit (from above)' in v. 5."[5] In 1:12–13 the narrator spoke of being "born of God." This birth is not the result of human procreation, human decision, or the will of a husband. It is altogether different from natural birth. The implied reader understands this critical distinction and also understands that some form of "rebirth" is implied here.

The interpretation set forth here recognizes that these two potential meanings for *anōthen* lie at the heart of the

3. This phrase has also proven difficult for translation committees. The NASB translates the phrase as "born again" without explanation or nuance; the NSRV translates it as "born from above" with a note indicating that "born anew" might also be an appropriate translation. The ESV, NIV, and NLT render the phrase as "born again" but provide a note indicating it might also be translated "from above." The CEV translates the phrase as "born from above" in vv. 3 and 7 without explanation. The NAB also translates the phrase as "born from above" in vv. 3 and 7 but provides an explanatory note giving the possible meanings for *anōthen*.

4. Moloney, *Gospel of John*, 98.

5. Ibid.

misunderstanding in this first exchange between Jesus and Nicodemus. A simplistic, overly literal understanding will not only create confusion in Nicodemus but will provide Jesus narrative space to explain his mission further, both to Nicodemus and the reader. In the verses that follow, Jesus will draw an even clearer connection between what it means to be born of God (1:13) and born *anōthen* (3:3).

B. Conversation, Part 2 (vv. 4–8). Having misunderstood Jesus' statement in v. 3 Nicodemus speaks again. In what appears to be an absurd instance of misunderstanding, Nicodemus now poses two questions: (1) "How is it possible for a man to be born when he is old?" (v. 4a); (2) "He cannot enter into his mother's womb a second time and be born again, can he? (v. 4b). The use of "a second time" (Greek: *deuteros*) confirms that Nicodemus has understood *anōthen* in the strictly literal sense of "again." Like many characters who will appear throughout the narrative, Nicodemus's overemphasis on the literal causes him to miss the point behind Jesus' words. On this point, Moloney comments that

> [Nicodemus] responds to Jesus in terms he can grasp. The concrete experience of "a second time" is within his comprehension but physically impossible. A rebirth "from above" is beyond his control and is thus simply ignored. Jesus' words to Nicodemus combine both the horizontal experience of time and the vertical experience of the inbreak of God. Nicodemus's response is limited to the horizontal, and he does not even raise the question of seeing the kingdom of God.[6]

Nicodemus's failure to understand the first element of Jesus' statement (being born *anōthen*; i.e., being "reborn from above") causes him to ignore completely the second element (seeing the kingdom of God). In his second comment

6. Moloney, *Belief in the Word*, 130.

to Nicodemus, Jesus continues to emphasize *spiritual rebirth* as a means to seeing the kingdom: "Amen amen I say to you, unless a person is born of water and spirit he will not be able to enter the kingdom of God" (v. 5). With the exception of two phrases, Jesus' first reply to Nicodemus is repeated verbatim. The parallels and differences are listed in the table below:

TABLE 7.4

Jesus' First Response to Nicodemus ***John 3:3***	**Jesus' Second Response to Nicodemus** ***John 3:5***
"Amen, amen I say to you"	"Amen, amen I say to you"
"Unless one is born *from above*"	"Unless one is born *of water and spirit*"
"he will not be able to *see*"	"he will not be able to *enter into*"
"the kingdom of God"	"the kingdom of God"

In Jesus' second reply, "born *from above*" is replaced by "born *of water and spirit*," and "*to see* the kingdom of God" is replaced by "*to enter into* the kingdom of God." While it is generally held among commentators that "see" and "enter" are used somewhat synonymously here, numerous questions are raised about the interpretation of the phrase "of water and spirit" (v. 5).

Some scholars see two different births implied by the phrase "of water and spirit." The first birth is thought to be physical and water is understood as a reference to either amniotic fluid or semen. The second birth, as implied by the use of the word "spirit" (Greek: *pneuma*), is a spiritual birth. Thus, one must first be born into the world by natural means and then experience a spiritual rebirth. Since the following verse reads, "What is born of flesh is flesh and what is born of spirit is spirit," those who argue for this interpretation regard the references to "flesh" and "spirit" as further confirmation that two births are in view in v. 5. However, there are at least three problems with this interpretation.

First, references to natural birth as "from water," are scarce in ancient sources and appear in texts written much later than the NT. In addition, if natural birth were in view here, one might expect "born of blood" (which is used in reference to natural birth in 1:13) rather than "born of water."

A second problem for this interpretation is that the passage shifts to a focus on "spirit" in the remaining verses (cf. vv. 6–9) whereas "water" is not mentioned again. This shift indicates that the idea of "spirit" is more prominent for the author's theological purposes.

A third objection to this interpretation is likely the most decisive. The Greek construction in view here argues against the presence of two distinct ideas. The structure of the phrase "born of water and spirit" usually indicates a compound object of the preposition, strongly suggesting *one idea* and therefore the focus on a *singular birth*. In light of these objections it seems best to argue that one birth is envisioned by the phrase "born of water and spirit." While there may have been baptismal significance at some level behind this phrase, there is more here than simply a veiled reference to the importance of baptism for John's community. The preferred interpretation of this verse understands the phrase "born of water and spirit" as a reference to new birth where cleansing and renewal are emphasized. The connection between spirit and water has already been hinted at in the words of John the Baptist regarding baptism by water and the spirit (see 1:26, 32–33); here that connection is made more concrete. In this way, the rebirth envisioned by Jesus reflects some of the important eschatological traditions of the OT.[7] Hence, birth by means of "water and spirit" is characterized by inner cleansing, spiritual renewal, and the ability to experience the kingdom in the present through association with Jesus. However, Nicodemus fails to understand once again, as the third stage of his conversation with Jesus will reveal (cf. v. 9).

From a literary perspective this interpretation makes the most sense in the context of Jesus' first conversation with a member of the Jewish leadership. Jesus speaks to Nicodemus in terms he cannot understand ("born from above") and in terms he should understand but does not ("born of water and spirit"). That Nicodemus fails to understand the imagery of his own Hebrew Scriptures further heightens the portrait of his incomprehension.

Jesus continues his explanation to Nicodemus by commenting: "What is born of flesh is flesh (Greek: *sarx*), and what is born of spirit is spirit (Greek: *pneuma*)" (v. 6). Rather than drawing a contrast between "water" and "spirit" as some have suggested, this verse contrasts natural birth and spiritual birth. Nicodemus has failed to understand that birth from above is different from natural birth. Natural birth was described in 1:13 as "of the will of the flesh

7. In the Hebrew Bible, the "spirit" is God's life-giving principle (see Gen 2:17; 6:3; Job 34:14) and some looked forward to the pouring out of God's spirit at the end of the age (Joel 2:28) as a repository of blessing (Isa 32:15–20; 44:3; Ezek 39:29). Water is also used in conjunction with the spirit to communicate cleansing and renewal.

(Greek: *sarx*)" and therefore it is significant that the term flesh is used here to connote natural birth once again. For John there are two births: a natural birth characterized by human volition and insight, and a spiritual birth characterized by renewal and cleansing.

In v. 7 Jesus continues his second reply to Nicodemus: "Do not be amazed that I said to you (singular), 'you (plural) must be born from above.'" In vv. 3, 5 Jesus spoke to Nicodemus exclusively in the singular. Here, however, he switches from the singular to the plural, indicating that he is speaking to Nicodemus about the implications of this teaching for a wider group. While this statement may have carried significance for the original readers of John, within the story the switch to the plural likely reflects a reply to Nicodemus's earlier use of the third person plural "we know" in v. 2a. Therefore the necessity of spiritual rebirth is not for Nicodemus alone but for those he claims to represent. As the story advances it becomes clear that Nicodemus moves closer and closer to this spiritual rebirth (see 7:45–52; 19:38–42), while those he represents (the Pharisees, the rulers, and *hoi Ioudaioi*) move further and further away.

Inasmuch as Jesus uses imagery that should be familiar to Nicodemus, there is an expectation that he ought to understand Jesus' words about being born of water and spirit. However, there is also a sense in which this birth is shrouded in mystery. This recognition brings about the intentional wordplay in Jesus' statement about the blowing of the wind: "The wind blows wherever it will, and you hear its sound but do not know where it comes from or where it is going" (v. 8ab). Just as the blowing of the wind (Greek: *pneuma*) is unpredictable and mysterious, so it is with those who are born of the Spirit (Greek: *pneuma*). Their origins and destination are unpredictable and mysterious to those of natural birth, who perceive reality only from the perspective of the flesh. The sound generated by the wind may also be an implicit reference to the voice of the Spirit. This observation deepens the sense of mystery drawn by the connection between the blowing of the wind and those born of the Spirit.

C. Conversation, Part 3 (vv. 9–12). In v. 9 Nicodemus speaks for the third and final time in this conversation. As in v. 4, he responds with a question that reveals the depths of his misunderstanding: "How can these things be?" Nicodemus began with sincere but contrived praise (v. 2b), then progressed to a question laden with misunderstanding (v. 4), and finally expresses complete bewilderment (v. 9). His final question shows that he still perceives Jesus from the perspective of the flesh. The irony here is rich: the ordinary reader understands religious truths that the leading religious authority cannot.

As in his previous two responses, Jesus again answers with a double amen statement, but not before expressing wonderment at Nicodemus's incomprehension: "Are you the teacher of Israel and yet you do not understand these things?" (v. 10). Jesus' identification of Nicodemus as "*the* teacher of Israel" is both a reminder to the reader that Nicodemus holds a significant place in the religious hierarchy of Israel and an ironic allusion to Nicodemus's earlier confession that Jesus is a teacher sent from God.

Following the pattern of vv. 3 and 5, Jesus responds to Nicodemus for a third time in v. 11: "We speak what we know and testify about what we have seen, but you (plural) do not receive our testimony." The second person plural plays an important role here. Like the reference to Nicodemus being "*the* teacher of Israel," Jesus' use of "we know" is an ironic allusion to Nicodemus's earlier confession in v. 2 ("*we know* that you are a teacher sent by God"). Nicodemus does not comprehend the substance of Jesus' testimony and therefore fails to receive his teaching. Likewise, Nicodemus's fellow Jewish leaders will fail to receive Jesus' teaching, confirming what the reader has already learned in the Prologue: "He came to his own place and his own people did not receive him" (1:11).

To this point, Jesus has been speaking of elemental earthly matters (v. 12a); if Nicodemus has been unable to grasp these basic truths, how will it be possible for him to grasp the heavenly things (v. 12b) about which Jesus has yet to speak? This supposed master of the Torah has failed to appreciate Jesus' teaching on what it means to be spiritually reborn. With this final question, Jesus states explicitly what the reader has witnessed throughout the conversation. The educated and respected Jewish leader who should be a sympathetic hero in the reader's estimation is instead shown to be a paradigm of misunderstanding.

II. Explaining Jesus' Words (3:13–21)

As mentioned previously, one of the distinctive features of John's Gospel is the existence of extended theological discourses. Unlike the Synoptic Gospels, where Jesus speaks primarily in parables, John's Jesus spends a great deal of narrative space explaining his origins, identity, and mission to the reader. The narrator also occasionally steps in to clarify Jesus' words further. In this portion of ch. 3, we have both an explanation from Jesus (vv. 13–15) and an expansion by the narrator (vv. 16–21).

A. Jesus Clarifies His Teaching (vv. 13–15). Jesus now begins to explain—contradicting the tradition that Israel's prophets had ascended to heaven to learn the secrets they revealed—that "no one has ascended into heaven except the one who came down from heaven, the Son of Man" (v. 13). This is a rather circuitous way for Jesus to speak about himself, though the reader understands full well what he means. Having read the Prologue, the reader is aware that Jesus is the one who existed with God prior to the creation of the world. The reader also knows that Jesus is the one who came down from heaven. He is the only one to have stood in the presence of God and the only one authorized to descend to earth. As such, he is the bearer of the full revelation of God. This is the first time in John that Jesus openly discusses his status as the revealer of God to humanity, though the reader has been aware of this since the opening verses.

The implied reader of John's Gospel has already heard the story of Jesus, but is being exposed to this version for the first time. The reader is thus aware of Jesus' impending death, but is still learning how this fits within John's understanding of Jesus. Verses 14–15 create a unique parallel that is not seen elsewhere in the NT—a comparison of the serpent in the wilderness that Moses "lifted up" with the Son of Man who will also be "lifted up." Jesus says, "And just as Moses lifted up the serpent in the wilderness, so must the Son of Man be lifted up, that whoever believes in him may have eternal life." Numbers 21 recounts the story of YHWH sending poisonous snakes upon his people for complaining against Moses and against the provisions of God. When the serpents emerge they begin to bite the Israelites, many of whom die. The Israelites once again turn to Moses and ask him to pray that YHWH would deliver them from serpents.

The solution provided in answer to Moses's prayer is found in 21:8–9:

> [YHWH speaking] "Make a poisonous serpent, and set it on a pole; and everyone who is bitten shall look at it and live." So Moses made a serpent of bronze, and put it upon a pole; and whenever a serpent bit someone, that person would look at the serpent of bronze and live.

John intends to draw a comparison between the salvific nature of looking upon the serpent in the wilderness and looking upon the crucified Jesus.

The Greek word used to describe this "lifting up" in both instances is also unique to John. The LXX (see table 2.1) rendering of Num 21 indicates that Moses created the serpent and "stood it on a sign," with nothing said about the actual "lifting up" of the serpent. Therefore, John's insertion of the verb *hypsoō* ("to lift up") in reference to the serpent (*hypsōsen*) and Jesus (*hypsōthēnai*) is intended to reinforce an important element of the gospel's theology of the cross. The term *hypsoō* can mean to "lift up" or "raise high" but can also be used in the figurative sense of "to exalt" or "enhance one's fame, position, or power." The Gospel of John is the only one of the four canonical gospels to present Jesus' death as his "exaltation." Jesus' lifting up on the cross will serve as the means by which God glorifies Jesus and exalts him before the world; all who identify with this exalted Jesus—like those who identified with the bronze serpent—will find life.

B. The Narrator Clarifies Jesus' Teaching (vv. 16–21). This section begins with John 3:16, what may be the most well-known verse in the entire NT. Because this verse is so often stripped of its context and inserted into the popular culture, it will be important to consider it within the framework of Jesus' encounter with Nicodemus and the gospel as a whole.

While some translations retain the quotation marks (or red letters) for this verse—thereby indicating that Jesus' words continue—it is probably better to read this as the voice of the narrator.[8] The theme of salvation was introduced in the previous verse, through the voice of Jesus. The narrator now takes an opportunity to develop this theme in greater detail. God loves the world and has provided for its salvation. This expression of the universal saving will of God recalls the words of 1:10–11, in which Jesus comes to his own place and his own people reject him. Further, the affirmation that "everyone who believes may have eternal life" recalls the next two verses of the Prologue—1:12–13—in which those who "believe in his name" will become children of God. Thus, what it means to be a child of God is expanded here in v. 16; the reader learns that having authority to be a child of God also means gaining eternal life.

Verses 17–18 begin to comment more specifically on the mission of Jesus. We know that he has come to reveal the Father to humanity. Part of this revelation is bound up in the salvation-condemnation dichotomy. Jesus came not to condemn the world but to save it. Condemnation is an existential reality that can only be overcome by believing in Jesus' name. These verses are an implicit call to decision. One can access the salvation God offers through belief in God's Son; otherwise, one is condemned by default.

Nicodemus left the conversation in both literal and metaphorical darkness, but the narrator wants to ensure that the reader gets the point. Using previous themes from the Prologue in vv. 19–21, the narrator seeks to emphasize for readers the power of decision as it relates to the identity of Jesus. With emphasis on "light," "life," "love,"

8. See footnote 1, above.

and "darkness" (see 1:4–8, 10–11), the narrator expounds further on the salvation-condemnation dichotomy. Verses 19–20 affirm what the proleptic comments in 1:9–11 announced at the beginning of the narrative: the light has come into the world, but people loved darkness more than the light. Through their evil deeds, they reject the Son, the "light of humanity" and choose darkness which leads to condemnation. On the other hand, those who practice the truth show evidence of their love for the light. This proper response to the revelation of God will inevitably result in salvation. The emphasis here is not on the sovereign acts of God, but rather the response of humanity that has been enlightened through God's revelation in Jesus.

CONCLUSION

Jesus' conversation with Nicodemus revisits important themes from the Prologue while expanding them in a way that causes the implied reader to learn new things. As stated earlier, the implied reader already knows a great deal more than the characters in the story, but is still in a position to progress in knowledge as the story unfolds. As God continues to be revealed to humanity, Jesus teaches that he is the great dividing line in history. As the purveyor of life, he has come to offer a universal salvation. As the light of humanity, he has come to expose the deeds of darkness and invite all men and women into God's light. The way to condemnation is found through rejecting the Son and persisting in darkness. While Nicodemus misunderstands Jesus' teaching and walks away bewildered, the narrator wants to be sure that the reader has clarity about Jesus, and is in a position to believe in the one who came down from heaven, the Son of Man.

Chapter 8

POSTSCRIPT

READING JOHN THEOLOGICALLY?

THROUGHOUT THIS BOOK I have tried to focus primarily on literary and historical concerns while leaving theological questions to the reader. However, this entire project is driven by the recognition that people continue to read the Gospel of John because it holds theological significance for them in the present day. Thus, it would be premature to conclude this book without briefly considering the question: "Does the Gospel of John open legitimate theological questions for contemporary readers?" I have already argued that the Fourth Gospel has proven foundational both for ancient and modern expressions of Christianity, so the answer to this question must necessarily be found at the intersection of three axes: (1) John's historical situation in a first-century context, (2) the major concerns, categories, and iterations of Christianity throughout the centuries, and (3) the contemporary context(s) of real readers. Keeping these three contexts in conversation with one another will ground our theological discussions historically and help prevent theological missteps of the past.

The Gospel of John is an inherently theological document with an unabashed interest in grand conversations about God, humanity, the world, the relationship between flesh and spirit, and the life that is found in Christ, both within this world and beyond. However, these universal and seemingly positive concerns are placed into sharp relief by the presence of more parochial theological concerns like sectarianism, exclusivity, and an ethical agenda that is limited to the imperatives of love and belief. What can we say about an ancient text that provides an abundance of material—both helpful and potentially problematic—for thinking about theology in a contemporary setting? Stephen Barton expresses the problem in this way:

> Given the dualism of the Gospel of John, how may this Gospel be appropriated in a theologically responsible way in the context of the cultural pluralism characteristic of (late- or post-) modernity? More generally: can we still *hear* a text whose particularities of language, form and content—all deeply moulded by the historical circumstances in which it took shape—seem to place the text at such a distance from the ideas and values of the contemporary world?[1]

In other words, since we cannot assume a one-to-one correspondence between the dualistic understanding of reality presented in the Fourth Gospel and the realities of living in the modern world, is there a legitimate way for contemporary Christians to move forward while appropriating the theology of the Gospel of John? The ultimate answer to this question must be rooted in the abiding belief that despite its occasionally limited focus, the Gospel of John ultimately speaks *about God* and *to humanity* in ways that remain universally important. This book has attempted to provide a historical and literary framework necessary for a

1. Barton, "Johannine Dualism and Contemporary Pluralism," 3, italics in original.

responsible reading of the Gospel of John. Let those who desire to use the Fourth Gospel in the context(s) of their theological reflection remain aware of both the possibilities and the difficulties, and move forward with an imagination worthy of John's theological vision and a sensitivity to frailty of the human experience.

REFLECTION:

1. What contemporary concerns (personal, social, ecclesial, global, ethical) are raised by an awareness of John's historical situation and distinctive literary presentation of Jesus' life and vocation?

2. Identify some ways—both useful and potentially harmful—of doing theology with the Gospel of John in our contemporary contexts.

BIBLIOGRAPHY

Allison, Dale. *The Historical Christ and the Theological Jesus*. Grand Rapids: Eerdmans, 2009.

Ball, David Mark. *'I Am' in John's Gospel: Literary Function, Background, and Theological Implications*. JSNT Supplement Series 124. Sheffield: Sheffield Academic, 1996.

Barton, Stephen C. "Johannine Dualism and Contemporary Pluralism." In *The Gospel of John and Christian Theology*, edited by Richard Bauckham and Carl Mosser, 3–18. Grand Rapids: Eerdmans, 2008.

Bauckham, Richard, ed. *The Gospels for All Christians: Rethinking the Gospel Audiences*. Grand Rapids: Eerdmans, 1998.

Blomberg, Craig. "The Gospels for Specific Communities *and* All Christians." In *The Audience of the Gospels: The Origin and Function of the Gospels in Early Christianity*, edited by Edward W. Klink III, 111–33. Library of New Testament Studies 353. London: T. & T. Clark, 2010.

Brown, Raymond E. *The Gospel according to John*. 2 vols. Anchor Bible 29, 29a. New York, Doubleday, 1966–1971.

———. *An Introduction to the Gospel of John*. Edited by Francis J. Moloney. Anchor Bible Reference Library. New York: Doubleday, 2003.

Bultmann, Rudolf. *The Gospel of John: A Commentary*. Translated by G. R. Beasley-Murray et al. Philadelphia: Westminster, 1971.

Carson, D. A. "Understanding Misunderstandings in the Fourth Gospel." *Tyndale Bulletin* 33 (1982) 59–91.

Carter, Warren. *John and Empire: Initial Explorations*. New York: T. & T. Clark, 2008.

Cohen, Shaye J. D. *From the Maccabees to the Mishnah*. 3rd ed. Louisville: Westminster John Knox, 2014.

Coloe, Mary L., and Tom Thatcher, eds. *John, Qumran, and the Dead Sea Scrolls*. SBL Early Judaism and Its Literature 32. Atlanta: Society of Biblical Literature, 2011.

Danielou, Jean. *Philo of Alexandria*. Translated by James G. Colbert. Eugene, OR: Cascade, 2014.

Danker, F. W., et al., eds. *Greek-English Lexicon of the New Testament and Other Early Christian Literature*. 3rd rev. ed. Chicago: University of Chicago Press, 2001.

De Jonge, Marinus. *Jesus: Stranger from Heaven and Son of God; Jesus Christ and the Christians in Johannine Perspective*. SBL Sources for Biblical Study 11. Missoula: Scholars, 1977.

Dunn, James D. G. "Let John Be John." In *Das Evangelium und die Evangelien*, edited by Peter Stuhlmacher, 309–39. Wissenschaftliche Untersuchungen zum Neuen Testament 28. Tubingen: Mohr, 1983.

Hylen, Susan. *Imperfect Believers: Ambiguous Characters in the Gospel of John*. Louisville: Westminster John Knox, 2009.

Keener, Craig S. *The Gospel of John: A Commentary*. 2 vols. Grand Rapids: Baker, 2003.

Klink, Edward, III, ed. *The Audience of the Gospels: The Origin and Function of the Gospels in Early Christianity*. Library of New Testament Studies. London: T. & T. Clark, 2010.

———. "The Gospel Community Debate: State of the Question." *Currents in Biblical Research* 3.1 (2004) 60–85.

———. *The Sheep of the Fold: The Audience and Origin of the Gospel of John*. Society of New Testament Studies Monograph Series 141. Cambridge: Cambridge University Press, 2007.

Law, Timothy Michael. *When God Spoke Greek: The Septuagint and the Making of the Christian Bible*. Oxford: Oxford University Press, 2013.

Levine, Amy-Jill. *A Misunderstood Jew: The Church and the Scandal of the Jewish Jesus*. San Francisco: HarperSanFrancisco, 2006.

Martyn, J. Louis. *History and Theology in the Fourth Gospel*. 3rd ed. Louisville: Westminster John Knox, 2003.

Meeks, Wayne. "'Am I a Jew?' Johannine Christianity and Judaism." In *Christianity, Judaism, and Other Greco-Roman Cults*, edited by Jacob Neusner, 1:163–85. Leiden: Brill, 1975.

———. "The Man from Heaven in Johannine Sectarianism." *Journal of Biblical Literature* 91 (1972) 44–72.

Michaels, J. Ramsey. *The Gospel of John*. New International Commentary on the New Testament. Grand Rapids: Eerdmans, 2010.

Moloney, Francis J. *Belief in the Word: Reading John 1–4*. Minneapolis: Fortress, 1993. Repr., Wipf & Stock, 2004.

———. *The Gospel of John*. Sacra Pagina 4. Collegeville: Liturgical, 2000.

O'Rourke, John J. "Asides in the Gospel of John." *Novum Testamentum* 21 (1979) 210–19.

Pyle, William T. "Understanding the Misunderstanding Sequences in the Gospel of John." *Faith and Mission* 11 (1994) 26–47.

Reinhartz, Adele. "Judaism in the Gospel of John." *Interpretation* 63 (2009) 382–93.

Richard, Earl. "Expressions of Double Meaning and Their Function in the Gospel of John." *New Testament Studies* 31 (1985) 96–112.

Richey, Lance Byron. *Roman Imperial Ideology and the Gospel of John*. Catholic Biblical Quarterly Monograph Series 43. Washington, DC: Catholic Biblical Association, 2007.

Skinner, Christopher W., "Another Look at the Lamb of God." *Bibliotheca Sacra* 161 (2004) 89–104.

———. *Characters and Characterization in the Gospel of John*. Library of New Testament Studies 461. London: Bloomsbury / T. & T. Clark, 2013.

———. "John's Gospel and the Roman Imperial Context: An Evaluation of Recent Proposals." In *Jesus Is Lord, Caesar Is Not: Evaluating Empire in New Testament Studies*, edited by Scot McKnight and Joseph B. Modica, 116–29. Downers Grove: InterVarsity, 2013.

———. "'Son of God' or 'God's Chosen One' (John 1:34)? A Narrative-Critical Solution to a Text-Critical Problem." *Bulletin for Biblical Research*. Forthcoming 2015.

Smiga, George M. *The Gospel of John Set Free: Preaching Without Anti-Judaism*. New York: Paulist, 2008.

Tenney, Merrill C. "The Footnotes of John's Gospel." *Bibliotheca Sacra* 117 (1960) 350–64.

Thatcher, Tom. "A New Look at Asides in the Fourth Gospel." *Bibliotheca Sacra* 151 (1994) 428–39.

———. *Greater than Caesar: Christology and Empire in the Fourth Gospel*. Minneapolis: Fortress, 2008.

Watty, William. "The Significance of Anonymity in the Fourth Gospel." *Expository Times* 90 (1979) 209–12.

Yee, Gale A. *Jewish Feasts and the Gospel of John*. Zaccheus Studies: New Testament. Wilmington, DE: Glazier, 1989.

FURTHER READING

1. Longer Introductory Works:

Anderson, Paul N. *The Riddles of the Fourth Gospel: An Introduction to John*. Minneapolis: Fortress, 2011.

Brown, Raymond E. *An Introduction to the Gospel of John*. Edited by Francis J. Moloney. Anchor Bible Reference Library. New York: Doubleday, 2003.

Culpepper, R. Alan. *Anatomy of the Fourth Gospel: A Study in Literary Design*. Philadelphia: Fortress, 1983.

———. *The Gospel and Letters of John*. Interpreting Biblical Texts. Nashville: Abingdon, 1998.

Kysar, *John, the Maverick Gospel*. 3rd ed. Louisville: Westminster John Knox, 2007.

2. Classic Commentaries:

Barrett, C. K. *The Gospel according to St. John: An Introduction with Commentary and Notes on the Greek Text*. 2nd ed. Philadelphia: Westminster, 1978.

Hoskyns, Edwin C. *The Fourth Gospel*. Edited by Francis Noel Davey. London: Faber & Faber, 1940.

Schnackenburg, Rudolf. *The Gospel according to St. John*. 3 vols. Translated by K. Smyth. London: Burns & Oates, 1968–1982.

3. More Recent Commentaries:

Brant, Jo-Ann A. *John*. Paideia Commentaries on the New Testament. Grand Rapids: Baker, 2011.

Keener, Craig S. *The Gospel of John: A Commentary*. 2 vols. Grand Rapids: Baker, 2003.

Lincoln, Andrew T. *The Gospel according to Saint John*. Black's New Testament Commentary. London: Continuum, 2005.

Moloney, Francis J. *Glory Not Dishonor: Reading John 13–21*. Minneapolis: Fortress, 1998. Repr., Wipf & Stock, 2004.

———. *Signs and Shadows: Reading John 5–12*. Minneapolis: Fortress, 1996. Repr., Wipf & Stock, 2004.

Smith, D. Moody. *John*. Abingdon New Testament Commentaries. Nashville: Abingdon, 1999.

4. Miscellaneous:

Brown, Raymond E. *The Community of the Beloved Disciple: The Life, Loves, and Hates of an Individual Church in New Testament Times*. New York: Paulist, 1979.

Culpepper, R. Alan, and C. Clifton Black, eds. *Exploring the Gospel of John: In Honor of D. Moody Smith*. Louisville: Westminster John Knox, 1996.

Dodd, C. H. *Historical Tradition in the Fourth Gospel*. Cambridge: Cambridge University Press, 1963.

———. *The Interpretation of the Fourth Gospel*. Cambridge: Cambridge University Press, 1965.

Donahue, John R., ed. *Life in Abundance: Studies of John's Gospel in Tribute to Raymond E. Brown*. Collegeville: Liturgical, 2005.

Kelly, Anthony J., and Francis J. Moloney. *Experiencing God in the Gospel of John*. New York: Paulist, 2003.

Koester, Craig. *The Word of Life: A Theology of John's Gospel*. Grand Rapids: Eerdmans, 2008.

Kysar, Robert. *Voyages with John: Charting the Fourth Gospel*. Waco, TX: Baylor University Press, 2005.

Lee, Dorothy. *Flesh and Glory: Symbolism, Gender and Theology in the Gospel of John*. New York: Crossroad, 2002.

Moloney, Francis J. *Love in the Gospel of John: An Exegetical, Theological, and Literary Study*. Grand Rapids: Baker, 2013.

Reinhartz, Adele. *Befriending the Beloved Disciple: A Jewish Reading of the Gospel of John*. London: Continuum, 2002.

Smith, D. Moody. *John among the Gospels: The Relationship in Twentieth-Century Research*. Minneapolis: Fortress, 1992.

Stibbe, Mark W. G. *John as Storyteller: Narrative Criticism and the Fourth Gospel*. Society of New Testament Studies Monograph Series 73. Cambridge: Cambridge University Press, 1992.

Thatcher, Tom, ed. *What We Have Heard from the Beginning: The Past, Present, and Future of Johannine Studies*. Waco, TX: Baylor University Press, 2007.

———. *Why John Wrote a Gospel: Jesus-Memory-History*. Louisville: Westminster John Knox, 2006.